FISH

FISH

Inspiring fish recipes
for creative cooks

Claire Macdonald

BANTAM PRESS

LONDON · TORONTO · SYDNEY · AUCKLAND · JOHANNESBURG

TRANSWORLD PUBLISHERS
61–63 Uxbridge Road, London W5 5SA
a division of The Random House Group Ltd

RANDOM HOUSE AUSTRALIA (PTY) LTD
20 Alfred Street, Milsons Point, Sydney,
New South Wales 2061, Australia

RANDOM HOUSE NEW ZEALAND LTD
18 Poland Road, Glenfield, Auckland 10, New Zealand

RANDOM HOUSE SOUTH AFRICA (PTY) LTD
Isle of Houghton, Corner of Boundary Road & Carse O'Gowrie,
Houghton 2198, South Africa

RANDOM HOUSE PUBLISHERS INDIA PRIVATE LTD
301 World Trade Tower, Hotel Intercontinental Grand Complex,
Barakhamba Lane, New Delhi 110 001, India

Published 2006 by Bantam Press
a division of Transworld Publishers

A catalogue record for this book is available from the British Library.
ISBN 9780593055830 (from Jan 07)
ISBN 0593055837

Typeset in Univers by Falcon Oast Graphic Art Ltd.

Printed in Great Britain by Butler and Tanner, Frome, Somerset

10 9 8 7 6 5 4 3 2 1

Papers used by Transworld Publishers are natural, recyclable products made from wood grown
in sustainable forests. The manufacturing processes conform to the environmental regulations
of the country of origin.

For my aunt and godmother, Christine Canti, and my uncle, Gordon Canti, who love food and with whom I still find inspiration in discussion on all things food-related.

Acknowledgements

I would like to thank the following, with whom I work in one way or another each day in my life and who have each, directly or indirectly, contributed in no small part to this book:

Godfrey, my husband; Isabella and Tom Eveling; Minty Dallmeyer; Peter Macpherson and Glyn Musker; Jenny Alldridge; Maggie Pearlstine; Nicki Harris; Sally Gaminara; Katrina Whone; Rachel MacKinnon; Nicola MacKay.

Colour photographs

Contents

Introduction

F ISH IS FANTASTIC FOOD. Fish is fast food, convenience cooking – words most usually associated with vile hamburgers and deep-fried chicken wings. And fish is so very good for us; in fact, we are told that we should eat fish at least three times a week for healthy living. Yet fish still has a bad reputation with many people. I am convinced that this is the direct result of institutional fish cooking. I remember that we ate fish for lunch on Fridays at school, and the school smelled of fish for days afterwards; it must have been the same in other schools up and down the country! Also, I know that many people are afraid of finding a bone in a mouthful of fish. Then there are others who dislike the feel of raw fish, so they tend to avoid buying it to save themselves the necessity of handling it prior to cooking. And there are many who simply do not know what to do with fish if they do buy it. These people are unaware of the wide range of fish dishes, all of which are simply delicious, so easy, and suitable for every occasion and meal imaginable.

Over the twenty years since I last wrote a book on fish cooking, I have learnt so much more about this delicious subject. Fish has become far more sought after. It used to be the case that the only fish we ever put on our menu here at Kinloch was wild salmon.

These days we have one fish or shellfish first course, and one of our two main courses is always fish. Fish has become expensive, and fish is a contentious subject all over the UK, but especially so here in Scotland, because of the severe depletion of our fishing fleet – down now, as I write, to 120 vessels. There is so much misinformation about fish. For instance, a protective body was set up in 2005 listing the fish we should not buy because of the need to preserve their stocks. But this list includes haddock, stocks of which, at the time of writing, are at a thirty-year high. So how can we who know these things have faith in any utterance by such a body? And there are people who say that we should not buy cod. Yet these people seem not to realize that some cod will always appear on the fish merchant's slab (and given it is already dead, not to buy it seems a pointless gesture anyway!) because cod is a by-catch of prawns.

I have a profound respect for fishermen and for fish merchants. I feel they are dealt a continued series of blows by politicians, and above all else I would vote for a politician, of whatever party, who aimed to get back our waters for British fishing – like Iceland has. Fishing is such a part of the life of the great island which is Britain, and the fact that the best fish and shellfish in the world are to be caught around the coasts of the UK, especially around Scotland, is proved by the keenness with which our waters are fished by the French and Spanish. And, incidentally, so deep in our psyche is the sea surrounding this island (not just Skye – I mean Great Britain) that when a fishing vessel gets into danger there is no hesitation in mounting the rescue – lifeboat and air–sea helicopter rescues when necessary – and our government is never recompensed for the cost of these rescues.

Several years ago our fresh fish was delivered to us whole, and we cleaned (gutted), filleted and, when necessary and depending on the recipe, skinned our own fish. These days we have a much easier life. Our fish arrives from one of our three fish merchants cleaned and filleted. The range of fish we use now is far more extensive than it was twenty years ago. For instance, it used to be the case that monkfish was thrown back when part of a catch, or it was bought by unscrupulous frozen food merchants who would chop up the monkfish, dip it in a sort of concrete-like batter and pass it off as scampi. This gives those of you still unfamiliar with the monkfish a good idea of its texture.

Within this book, I fervently hope, are recipes and talk about fish – a subject so near to my heart – that will for evermore dispel any fears or feelings of not being able to cope in those of you who have doubts. Hopefully these recipes will encourage more and more people to eat fish, realizing just how versatile and simple it is. And I very much hope to awaken in all who read this book an awareness of the hazards faced by those who bring fish from the sea to the shops.

But please read on, because I must tell you about fish and shellfish, methods of preservation, selecting fish, and a host of other things which will, I hope, be helpful and useful!

Choosing fresh fish

So much of value in assessing the freshness of fish lies in its appearance. Look at the eyes – eyes that seem to have shrunk in the sockets denote less than fresh fish. Fish should look firm, not dull and limp. Nearly all fish should be of the freshest. Large trawlers that immediately pack their catch in ice can give fish which is very fresh, even if it is two or three days old. There are, however, two types of fish that are better when not fresh caught. Skate is one – it tastes so much better 2–3 days old – and wild salmon is better aged by a couple of days; Godfrey maintains that this is because salmon is a game fish, and benefits from resting on a shelf in a cold larder before being cooked. So much ordinarily farmed salmon is stunned then bled to death that this ageing process simply does not apply to farmed fish.

If you have fish filleted and cleaned for you, ask the fishmonger or merchant to give you the bones – they are invaluable for making fish stock.

Smoked fish should **never** be a vivid, lurid yellow-orange, indicating dye. And, of course, smoked fish keeps for 2–3 days in the fridge. But if fish – or anything, for that matter – is in a polythene bag, it will not keep at all well, so open the bag and lay the fish on a large plate or plastic tray, covered with baking parchment. This will keep it so much better.

Cleaning and filleting fish

Most probably these days your fish seller will do the filleting and gutting for you. But there may be times when you catch your own fish, or are given fish whole, so this small section is for those occasions.

The most vital implement for this procedure is a really sharp knife, one with a long, thin blade.

To fillet a flat fish (halibut, plaice, sole) cut down either side of the backbone, working towards the outer sides and keeping as close to the bones as you can. There is no need to gut a flat fish before filleting.

To fillet a round fish, such as salmon, gut it first: cut up its belly in a straight line, scoop out the innards and wash the cavity under cold running water. Cut off the head and tail, then, grasping your very sharp knife firmly, cut down one side of the backbone along the bones, very carefully so as not to leave any more flesh on the bones than you can help. When you have one side off, repeat the process on the other side. Then, with the fish skin-side down on the work surface, cut the skin off by stroking the knife blade on it, held horizontally. This way you will get a skinned fillet of fish with no flesh whatever on the skin.

The first time you skin and fillet a fish it seems to take an age, but – as with most things in life – the more frequently you do it, the easier it becomes.

If you are filleting a big fish, like turbot or halibut, cut out the flesh from the cheeks – there is a surprising amount and it is supposed to be the best part of the fish!

When you want a fish whole and unskinned – and salmon is the perfect example – scrape off the scales under cold running water, working from the tail towards the head.

Freezing fish

In my book on fish twenty years ago I was rather keen on freezing fish. These days I am not – in fact, I really do not think that most fish freezes well at all. However, salmon is one fish which I think does not deteriorate after a brief (7–10 days') sojourn in the freezer. With other types of fish – notably hake and tuna – I can tell immediately if they have been frozen, by both their texture and their taste.

Smoking fish

Smoking is by far the best-known way of preserving fish. Smoked fish varies widely, from the delicate to the downright shoe-leather smoked, when it is hard to tell that the subject ever was fish in the first place. There are two forms of smoked fish:

Hot-smoking

When hot-smoked, fish are both smoked and lightly cooked at the same time. Arbroath Smokies are hot-smoked – they are haddock which have their heads severed, and the innards are removed through the hole left by cutting away the head; they are not split down. They are delicious – well, I love all smoked fish, providing that it has been smoked well. Then there is hot-smoked mackerel, which sometimes has crushed black peppercorns pressed over the fish as they hot-smoke. I think smoked mackerel is very good indeed – and it is a fish so rich in the valuable omega-3 oils that we should eat it as frequently as possible. And salmon and trout are both hot-smoked. When salmon is hot-smoked it is called by a number of names: 'roast' or 'flaky' to list just two. The best-known hot-smoke of salmon is the award-winning Salar, from South Uist. But all smokehouses will hot-smoke salmon, and all will have a slight variation. Hot-smoking, like cold-smoking, takes place over oak sawdust and shavings. It is perhaps stating the obvious, but fish which has been hot-smoked needs no further cooking, and yet it can be used in cooked recipes – for instance, hot-smoked salmon makes fishcakes which are infinitely more delicious than any plain salmon fishcakes. And hot-smoked salmon makes a luxurious kedgeree, combined with saffron and quails' eggs (see page 208).

Cold-smoking

When fish are cold-smoked they remain raw. The smoking takes place over oak sawdust or chips, as for hot-smoking, but the temperature in the smokehouse is lower. Cold-smoked fish include salmon (which we eat sliced wafer thin, and raw; in fact I loathe any recipe in which cold-smoked salmon is heated because I find it accentuates its oiliness); herring, which, when cold-smoked, become kippers and are one of life's great delicacies; haddock, whiting, cod and hake. And halibut and monkfish are to be found cold-smoked, sliced wafer thin and served on menus as *carpaccio*, just drizzled with olive oil and occasionally accompanied by a citrus-based salsa or a dressing. As the years pass, smokehouses become more innovative, which just makes life ever more interesting for those of us who love to eat – and cook!

Smoked salmon should not be hideously orange, just pale golden, tinged with apricot. Best of all I like it eaten with a squeeze of lemon juice and lots of black pepper, our granary bread and butter. But it is also delicious with cream cheese and bagels – the classic Jewish bagel and lox is my idea of the perfect breakfast, lunch or dinner. And thinly sliced brown bread, spread with butter and crushed walnuts which have been fried in butter, which is then rolled up and cut into small rounds makes an excellent and complementary taste and texture to eat with smoked salmon.

There is smoked salmon and smoked salmon. Wild smoked, or organically farmed smoked, is best. The smoked salmon we love is that from the Sleepy Hollow Smokehouse at Aultbea; from the Hebridean Smokehouse in North Uist; and from Craster, in Northumberland, who smoke perfectly delicious salmon. There are, of course, very many others, but these three are my favourites.

Before herring are kippered – smoked – they are dipped into a brine of 90 per cent salt solution for 20 minutes. They are then hung by their heads, in pairs on a stick, placed on a rack and cold-smoked overnight. There are different methods of cooking kippers – Godfrey prefers them grilled, I like to shallow-poach them in water.

When white fish is cold-smoked, it has much less time in its brine – barely 3–5 minutes before smoking.

Salting fish

These days, this method of preserving fish is encountered less often than it once was. But salt herring are a seasonal delicacy – probably unavailable in most of the country, but I urge you to try them if you ever get the chance. There is something very satisfying about a plate of salt herring eaten with plain boiled potatoes. The herring must first be soaked in cold water, then simmered in fresh water, with three changes of water as the fish cooks. Even then thirst seems an unavoidable aftermath of a meal of salt herring, but it is worth it! Herring that are to be salted are first cleaned but their roes are left in. The fish are then packed in barrels between layers of salt. In the side of the barrel there is a bung and 3–4 days after salting, the bung is removed, brine is poured into the barrel and the bung is replaced. This is done because, as the salt dissolves in the juices which seep from the fish, the level drops, leaving an airspace in which bacteria could breed. The barrel is then turned from time to time. Salt herring are ready to be eaten after 7 days.

And then I must tell you about red herring, which is not just the proverbial distraction, but a herring that has just spawned. These fish have a slit cut in their necks but are otherwise left whole and uncleaned. They are then salted, as for ordinary salt herring. When they are to be smoked, they are soaked overnight in fresh water and then hung at the top of the smokehouse for a whole month. You really have to love the salty smoky flavour to be able to enjoy a red herring!

Shellfish

Scallops

We buy our scallops shelled. But if you happen to get them still in their shells, don't be daunted by the thought of prising them loose, because there is a very quick and easy method, as shown to me by my friend and former fish merchant George Lawrie. Hold the scallop with the flat shell against the palm of your hand. Stick a long thin knife into the 'waist' of the shell, and cut firmly round – the meat will be left in the rounded shell. Remove the frilly bit round the very edges of the white meat, and the little dark grey tube at the side of the coral. Stab the coral to prevent it popping as it sears. There is your scallop, ready to cook.

Mussels

We have quantities of mussels growing on the rocks below our house, just there for the picking. We leave them overnight in a bucket of fresh water with a couple of handfuls of oatmeal. This is supposed to be eaten by the mussels, which then rid themselves of any grit inside their stomachs. I'm never quite sure if they really do this, but we give them the opportunity. Then the mussels need to be scrubbed well, under cold running water.

To cook, put them in a large saucepan with a tightly fitting lid, and add an equal quantity of water; I add 1.2 litres/2 pints water to 1.2 litres/2 pints mussels, which serves six people. To this I add 150ml/¼ pint white wine, a small onion, very finely chopped, and a handful of chopped parsley. Cover the pan and put over a moderately high heat, shaking it from time to time, for 7–10 minutes. Throw away any mussels that aren't open – these will have been dead before they were cooked, and so aren't safe to eat.

We also buy mussels from a mussel farm 2 miles from Kinloch. There they grow up ropes in deep water, which means they are never exposed to the sun at low tide, nor do they ingest grains of sand.

Prawns

The huge, succulent langoustines, which we are lucky enough to get, are also known as Norwegian lobsters, or Dublin Bay prawns. When they have their heads removed they can legitimately be called, under the Trades Descriptions Act, scampi tails. So, a prawn by any other name can only be a shrimp!

The answer to cooking all prawn-type shellfish is boiling water. Get a big pan of water boiling fast, then put your prawns in, and give them 45 seconds in the water to cook. Drain them at once. If they are at all overcooked they become mushy. Spread them flat to cool. To shell prawns, wait until they are cool enough to handle, squeeze them lengthwise, then break apart their shells and the curved, cooked body can be pulled out.

Lobster

You pay more to eat lobster on menus throughout the world than for any other item, and yet I personally prefer crab, langoustines and scallops – unless the lobster is really fresh. Lobster is only really good if it is brought from the sea to the pot. As they travel, lobsters release an enzyme which toughens them – overcooking also toughens them. Lobster is so often tough and chewy, and I also think the flavour of crab and scallops is much nicer. But I know that I am very much in the minority. Having said all that, I do really love fresh lobster, served simply, either cold with a good mayonnaise, or hot with melted butter, a squeeze of lemon juice and chopped chives.

Crab

I love crab, preferably eaten plain, with some good mayonnaise and brown bread. Godfrey loves both crab and lobster served hot, with rich sauces made with cream, brandy or cheese.

To cook crab, have ready a pan of boiling, salted water and plunge them in – this kills them instantly. Boil them for about 10–15 minutes to the half-kilo or the pound, then cool them on a tray. To shell a crab, stand it on its head with its big claws down, and press on the top of the shell with both your thumbs. This opens the shell so you can pull the body and claws away. Throw away the bundle of intestines and scoop any soft, creamy brown flesh from inside the shell into a bowl. On the body of the crab are the gills, known repulsively as the dead man's fingers; pull these out. Scoop and scrape the flesh from the body, then, with a large metal spoon bash the brown meat together. Here at Kinloch, when we have fresh crab on the menu, I serve the crabmeat just like this, on a bed of shredded lettuce with a tomato and garlic mayonnaise at the side.

Other fish

Fish divide into categories in two ways. One way is by shape. There are, roughly speaking, two shapes of fish: *Round fish*, including salmon, cod, herring, haddock, mackerel, bass, whiting, trout, red mullet and grey mullet, and many others. *Flat fish*, including turbot, sole, plaice, halibut and brill.

Another way of categorizing fish is by the texture of its flesh. There are soft fish, such as plaice, lemon sole, grey sole and haddock (although haddock is slightly less soft in texture than the others). These fish require very careful cooking, as they tend to fall apart if they are overcooked.

Then there are firmer-fleshed fish, such as turbot and halibut (both of which are also fairly gelatinous in texture), Dover sole, skate, cod and monkfish (which is very firm-fleshed). These fish stand up to cooking much better than the softer-fleshed varieties. They are suitable for using as kebabs, in barbecuing and for casseroles.

Some fish are much oilier than others – the one which immediately springs to mind is herring, which is also the most nutritious of all fish. Mackerel is also very oily, and so are salmon, pilchards and sardines, and swordfish.

Squid

Squid are delicious and not as difficult to clean as people think. Inside the body there is a feather-shaped blade of cartilage. If you grasp this firmly and pull, it comes out. Throw away the head, innards and ink sac. Then wash the squid well in running water both inside and out, and cut it into circles, reducing the tentacles to 4cm (1½-inch) lengths. The thing **not** to do with squid is to overcook it – a minute or two in olive oil and garlic is all it needs. If squid is left cooking for too long it becomes tough and very chewy – rather like overcooked liver or kidney.

Stock

Fish stock

This is well worth making. It doesn't take a minute to put together, and only 10 minutes to cook, but it makes such a difference to fish dishes.

In a saucepan, put 600 ml/1 pint each of dry white wine and water, any fish skin and bones, an onion, skinned and sliced, a carrot, chopped, a bay leaf, a few stalks of parsley and about 12 peppercorns. Bring the liquid to the boil and simmer for 10 minutes. Pour the stock into whatever dish you are going to cook the fish in and leave to cool. Put the filleted fish into the stock and cover with greaseproof paper to cook.

If you are making a dish where stock is not required, such as roasted monkfish, don't waste the trimmings – make up a fish stock and freeze it for later use.

Certain fish – turbot and skate in particular – make a very gelatinous stock, which can be useful for cold fish dishes.

Chicken stock

It may sound odd, but some of the recipes in this book contain chicken stock. This is usually where tinned fish is used, or where the fish used doesn't give you anything with which to make fish stock. Home-made chicken stock is best, but if you have none available a good stock substitute such as Marigold will do. Or make up some vegetable stock: just boil up a chopped onion, skin and all, with some carrot and any other vegetables to hand, except potato, for about an hour.

Fish soups

THE SOUPS IN THIS CHAPTER are mostly for use as first courses, but in some cases the recipe is suitable only as a main course because it would be just too filling to eat at the start of a lunch, supper or dinner. In some recipes I use a mixture of butter and oil, in others just butter. This is because some recipes (very few!) taste better with butter or olive oil alone. In the past I sometimes used flour to thicken soups. These days I never use anything other than potato as a thickener. You will see that almost all the soup recipes contain chopped parsley, or parsley and snipped chives. This is such a good way to flavour as well as to lift the colour and overall appearance of a soup. Very often the content of a soup would be altogether too beige without the herbs – for instance, the Jerusalem Artichoke and Scallop Soup (on page 40).

Soup is such a wonderful and varied dish, and within this chapter I hope that you will find inspiration and satisfaction.

Avocado soup with prawns

This is a special occasion soup for a hot day, and it is of the very best when the prawns are succulent and sweet langoustines. But other types of prawn can be used, of course, and the taste of prawns with avocados is such a good combination.

Serves 6

3 tbsps olive oil
2 onions, skinned and chopped quite small
900 ml/1½ pints chicken or vegetable stock
3 avocados, preferably the knobbly dark-skinned variety, which have the best flavour
juice of ½ lemon
½ tsp Tabasco
4 tbsps full fat crème fraîche
salt
black pepper
225 g/8 oz prawns, cooked (see page 21) and chopped
2 tbsps chopped parsley and snipped chives, mixed

Heat the olive oil in a saucepan and fry the chopped onions for several minutes, until they are quite soft and transparent-looking. Then add the stock, bring to the boil and simmer for 2–3 minutes. Take the pan off the heat, and cool the contents completely.

Meanwhile, cut each avocado in half and, with the point of a knife, flick out the stones. With a teaspoon, scoop the flesh from each avocado half, scraping inside the skins, where the strongest colour lies. Put the avocado flesh into the cold onions and stock. Add the lemon juice and Tabasco, then liquidize the contents of the pan to a smooth, light green soup. At the very end of liquidizing briefly whiz in the crème fraîche. Taste the soup, and add salt and black pepper to your liking – and more lemon juice too if you think it is needed. Stir the chopped prawns, chopped parsley and snipped chives through the soup. Store the soup in a covered container in the fridge until you are ready to serve it. There is no need for further garnish – the chopped prawns and the herbs are quite enough!

fish soups

Creamy smoked haddock soup

I have written and cooked various versions of this soup over the years, but this is, I think, the best of the lot. It is imperative that only the best smoked haddock is used – absolutely none of the vivid yellow-dyed stuff. And I think it is important to fry the onions and raw potatoes gently together in the butter and oil combination for as long as possible, stirring to prevent them sticking, before adding the smoked haddock milk. Somehow the result tastes much better than if the potatoes and onions cook in the milk. The tomatoes, parsley and nutmeg make this soup for me.

This is a filling soup and more worthy of being a main course in itself rather than a first course.

Serves 6

675 g/1½ lb smoked haddock
1.2 litres/2 pints milk and water mixed
50 g/2 oz butter and 1 tbsp olive oil
2 onions, skinned and chopped
3 medium-sized potatoes, peeled and chopped
a good grinding of nutmeg – about ½ teaspoon
plenty of black pepper (no salt: the fish tends to add enough)
3 tomatoes, skinned, halved, seeds scooped away, then diced thumbnail-size
2 heaped tbsps chopped parsley

Put the fish into a saucepan with the milk and water. Bring the liquid to simmering point. Simmer for 1 minute, then draw the pan off the heat and leave the fish to cool completely in the milk – as it does so, it will infuse the milk and water with its taste. When cooled, lift the fish out and carefully flake it, removing all the skin and the bones. Strain the liquid through a sieve into a large measure jug to make into the soup.

Melt the butter and heat it together with the olive oil in a large, heavy saucepan. Fry the chopped onions for 2–3 minutes before adding the chopped potatoes. Cook, over a moderate heat and stirring occasionally to prevent sticking, for 10 minutes. Then pour in the fish liquid, and season with nutmeg and pepper. Bring the liquid

Creamy smoked haddock soup

to simmering point and cook gently for 5–7 minutes. Make sure that the potato is quite soft by squishing a bit against the side of the pan with the back of your wooden spoon. Cool, and liquidize the contents of the saucepan.

Put the liquid back into a clean pan – at this stage you can, if it is more convenient, store it in a covered bowl in the fridge overnight – and reheat, adding the flaked fish and diced tomatoes 5 minutes before serving, and stirring in the chopped parsley just before serving. The longer the parsley sits in the hot soup the more it will change from its bright, fresh colour to a duller greyish green, and its flavour, too, diminishes.

Salmon, wild garlic and potato soup

Alexandra, our eldest daughter, lives in Austria, and they make delicious soup using their wild-growing garlic mixed with potatoes. We are lucky to have garlic growing around us in Skye, and I add cold leftover salmon to my garlic and potato soup. In the absence of wild garlic, use cultivated garlic and chives instead (wild garlic is milder by far than cultivated).

Serves 6

50 g/2 oz butter and 1 tbsp olive oil
1 onion, skinned and chopped
3 medium-sized potatoes, peeled and chopped
1.2 litres/2 pints fish or vegetable stock
3 whole bulbs of wild garlic (*or* 3 cloves of bought garlic and 2 tbsps snipped chives),
papery skin removed and the long stalks with their small bulbous ends chopped
salt, to taste
plenty of black pepper
a good grating of nutmeg
450 g/1 lb flaked cooked salmon
1 heaped tbsp chopped parsley

Melt the butter and heat it with the olive oil in a saucepan. Fry the chopped onion for 2–3 minutes before adding the chopped potatoes. Cook, stirring occasionally to prevent sticking, for 10 minutes. Pour in the stock and bring the liquid to simmering point. Add the garlic at this point and simmer gently for 4–5 minutes, till when you squish a piece of potato against the side of the pan with the back of your wooden spoon it is quite soft. The reason for adding the garlic towards the end of the cooking time is that its flavour almost disappears if it cooks for too long. Cool, then liquidize the contents of the pan.

Reheat in a clean saucepan, taste, and add salt accordingly, and pepper and nutmeg. Stir in the flaked salmon a few minutes before serving to heat it through, and add the chopped parsley just before serving to retain its vivid colour and taste.

Crab and rice soup

For this soup you can either use chicken stock, as in the recipe or, if you are using meat from whole crabs, make a stock from the crab shells and use that instead. As with the Creamy Smoked Haddock Soup (page 31), this crab soup is more useful as a main course – it is rather filling for a first course. The result will only be as delicious as it should be if the crab is the best quality – we are so lucky here in Skye, because we have access to local crab and the quality is unsurpassable.

Serves 6

75 g/3 oz butter
2 onions, skinned and diced very finely – ideally done in an onion dicer
75 g/3 oz basmati rice
1.2 litres/2 pints chicken stock
450 g/1 lb crabmeat, white and brown mixed
salt
freshly ground black pepper
a grating of nutmeg
2 tbsps chopped parsley

Melt the butter in a saucepan and fry the finely diced onion till it is very soft, transparent-looking and just beginning to turn golden at the edges. Do this over a moderate heat to prevent the butter burning. (This is one of very few recipes where I prefer to use only butter and not a combination of butter with olive oil.) Then stir in the rice, and pour in the stock. Simmer gently till the rice is cooked – 6–7 minutes. Stir in the crabmeat, taste, and season with salt, pepper and nutmeg. Just before serving, stir in the chopped parsley, which is present in this recipe as well as in most others for its taste but also for its colour.

fish soups

Mussel, onion and potato chowder

I used to add flour to the mussels and onions in this recipe, but a few years ago I decided that potatoes are a far better thickener than flour. They taste better. Mussels are so easy to buy these days, as they are very successfully farmed. The best are large, plump and orange-fleshed. Try to avoid those which are small and an anaemically pale straw colour.

Serves 6

1.2 litres/2 pints mussels
1.2 litres/2 pints cold water
1 onion, skinned and quartered
150 ml/¼ pint dry white wine

50 g/2 oz butter and 1 tbsp olive oil *For the soup*
2 onions, skinned and finely diced
3 potatoes, peeled and diced small (about the size of a thumbnail)
1.2 litres/2 pints of the mussels' cooking liquid
salt
black pepper
2 tbsps chopped parsley

Start by cooking the mussels – scrub them under running cold water and put them into a large saucepan with the water, quartered onion and white wine. Put a lid on the pan and, over a moderate heat, bring the liquid to a boil. Boil for 1 minute. Lift the lid and check that the mussels have opened – this means they are cooked. Throw away any unopened mussels because they were dead before cooking and there is no way to know how long they had been dead. You must be safe and just throw them out.

Meanwhile, melt the butter and heat it with the olive oil in another large pan. Fry the diced onion over a moderate heat for 2–3 minutes,

Mussel, onion and potato chowder

then add the diced potatoes and continue to cook for a further 10 minutes, stirring occasionally to prevent the mixture sticking. Strain the cooking liquid from the mussels into the onions and potatoes, and bring to a gentle simmer. Cook for 5 minutes, or until the potato is quite soft.

Meanwhile, take the mussels from their open shells, and throw away the shells. Taste the soup mixture, and add salt and pepper to your taste. Just before serving, put the mussels into the soup, let them heat through for a couple of minutes, then stir in the chopped parsley immediately before serving the soup to help keep its colour and taste bright and fresh.

Moules marinières

This soup or stew of mussels has no potatoes and the mussels are left and served in their shells. Try to buy large mussels. One of the joys of farmed mussels is that they need little cleaning. They are grown on ropes in deep sea where there is no danger of them being exposed by falling tides (see Introduction, page 20). They feed naturally, and are delicious and inexpensive.

Serves 6

3.6 litres/6 pints mussels, each scrubbed briefly under running cold water
4 fat garlic cloves, skinned and finely diced or chopped
900 ml/1½ pints water
300 ml/½ pint dry white wine
plenty of black pepper – you can add salt later if you think it is needed
2 tbsps chopped parsley

Put the scrubbed mussels into a large saucepan which has a tight-fitting lid. Add the garlic, water, white wine and pepper. Cover the pan with its lid and put it on a fairly high heat. Cook for 10 minutes, shaking the pan from time to time. Then stir in the chopped parsley – it is not easy to do this too thoroughly, but it will become distributed amongst the heap of mussels as you ladle them into the warmed soup plates. Serve, with a large bowl to receive the shells as the mussels are eaten. Be sure to warn guests to throw away any unopened mussels. Serve with chunks of warm bread, which, if you like, can be spread with garlic and parsley butter.

Langoustine bisque

This is a rich soup, luxurious in both taste and texture, yet using the shells from these succulent crustacea. It can be made a day in advance providing that it is kept in the fridge. It makes a perfect and elegant first course for a special occasion.

Serves 6

For the langoustine stock
2.4 litres/4 pints langoustine shells
1 onion, skinned and quartered
2 sticks of celery, chopped
150ml/¼ pint dry white wine
1.2 litres/2 pints water

6 cooked and shelled langoustines –
**   for garnish (see page 21 for cooking instructions)**
75 g/3 oz butter
2 onions, skinned and chopped
1 carrot and 1 leek, each peeled, trimmed and chopped quite small
2 potatoes, peeled and diced small
1 tbsp tomato purée
strained langoustine stock
4 tbsps brandy
salt, to taste
a grinding of black pepper
a grating of nutmeg
150 ml/¼ pint double cream

Put the ingredients for the langoustine stock into a large saucepan, cover the pan with its lid and, over a moderately high heat, cook for 10 minutes. Then cool the contents of the pan completely. Strain the contents, throwing away the shells and vegetables.

Melt the butter in a large saucepan and fry the chopped onions for 2–3 minutes, then add the chopped carrot and leek and the diced potatoes. Cook, stirring from time to time to prevent sticking, for 10 minutes. Then stir in the tomato purée, and pour in the langoustine stock. Bring the contents of the pan to a gentle simmer and cook for 10 minutes. Add the brandy, and bring back to the boil. Take the pan off the heat, cool and liquidize till very smooth and silky of texture – if the blades of your blender are not of the sharpest, sieve the liquidized soup to achieve a really smooth texture. Taste, and season with salt, pepper and nutmeg. Stir in the double cream – it must be double, to prevent any danger of curdling. Reheat, and serve, with a whole, shelled langoustine in each serving.

Jerusalem artichoke soup with seared scallops

This soup combines two most complementary flavours, that of scallops with Jerusalem artichokes. There is only one scallop in each serving, so this is perfectly delicious as a first course. On the other hand, if you add more than one scallop per person, it can be a main course in itself.

Serves 6

6 king scallops, with olive oil poured over them

For the soup 3 tbsps olive oil
2 onions, skinned and chopped
450 g/1 lb Jerusalem artichokes, each peeled and chopped
1.2 litres/2 pints chicken or vegetable stock
salt
black pepper
a grating of nutmeg
2 tbsps chopped parsley and snipped chives, mixed

Soak the scallops in olive oil for a couple of hours. Heat a sauté pan or a frying pan till very hot. Then lift each scallop and drop it into the very hot dry pan. Cook, without moving the scallops around in the pan, for 20 seconds before turning them to cook on their other sides. Set the seared scallops aside, on a plate.

Make the soup by heating the olive oil in a large saucepan and frying the onions in this for 2–3 minutes, until they are soft and transparent-looking. Then add the peeled and chopped artichokes. Stir them well together, then pour in the stock. Bring the liquid to simmer and cook gently for 15–20 minutes, or until when you squish a piece of artichoke against the side of the pan it is quite soft. Then

fish soups

cool the contents of the pan before liquidizing the soup to a smooth texture. Taste, and season with salt, pepper and a grating of nutmeg. The soup can be made and kept for up to 2 days providing that it is stored in the fridge in a covered container. It can be frozen for a limited time – no longer than 3 months.

Reheat the soup to serve, stirring the chopped parsley and snipped chives through the soup just before serving, and put a seared scallop in the bottom of each soup plate before ladling the soup over it. A seared scallop is easily cut with the side of a spoon, it is so soft. Only an overcooked fried scallop would be tough!

First courses lunch or supper

or savouries, er dishes

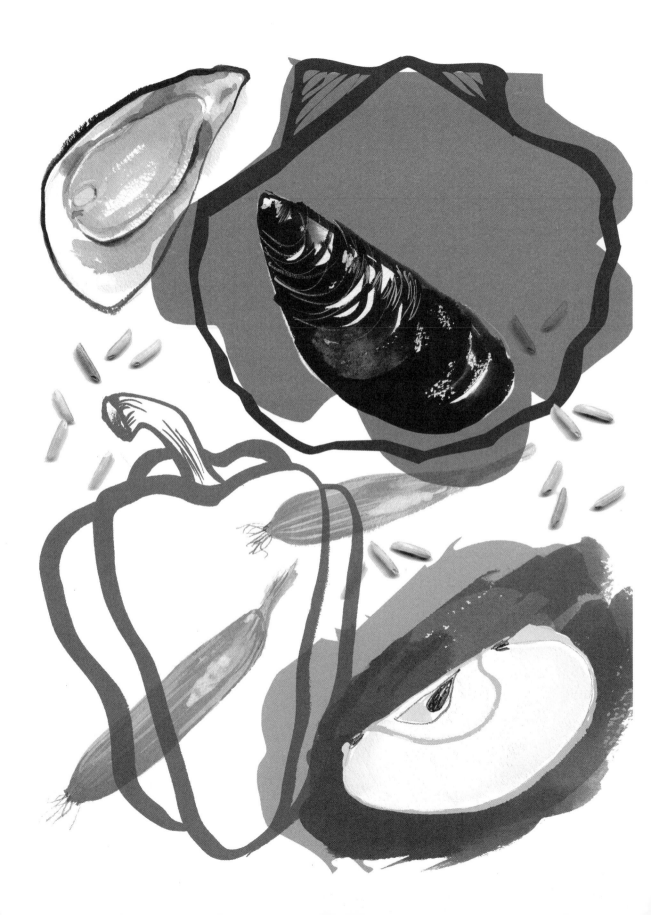

I N THIS CHAPTER THERE ARE many recipes which could be a main course for a lunch or supper, or which could be a first course or a savoury. In the introduction to each recipe I say if the recipe is suitable for other than a first course. There are many who still prefer a savoury finale to supper or dinner, rather than a pud, and within this chapter there are a few recipes which are ideal for either the beginning or the end of the meal. Fish is so quickly cooked, and therefore so convenient, that it makes an ideal subject for any course. It is what we do with the fish or shellfish which can take a small amount of time in preparation. Wherever such preparation can be done in advance, I will point it out in the recipe.

Smoked mackerel pâté

We can buy juicy and succulent smoked mackerel fillets pretty well any-where these days. It is a fish rich in omega-3 oils and therefore we should eat it as often as we can. Made into a pâté, it is useful and delicious for a variety of occasions. Here I intend it to be a first course, served with crisp Melba toast or toasted granary bread, but served in larger amounts it is very good as a main course for a lunch or supper dish, accompanied by a mixed-leaf salad dressed with mustard vinaigrette, along with bread or toast. It is also very good with lettuce leaves to fill buns for a picnic. Try adding fried chopped walnuts to the pâté if you like; they give a good contrasting crunch to its smooth texture. It can be made two days ahead providing that it is kept in the fridge, in a covered bowl. It doesn't freeze well, though – I don't think any fish pâté does.

Serves 6

4 smoked mackerel fillets, total weight approx. 450 g/1 lb
375 g/12 oz cream cheese (use Philadelphia Lite
    if you like, but the pâté will be much softer)
lots of black pepper
a dash of Tabasco
4 tbsps lemon juice (to cut the richness of the smoked mackerel)
2 tbsps chopped parsley

Flake the fish into a food processor, removing any bones you encounter. Add the cream cheese to the processor, and lots of black pepper – about 25 grinds. Whiz to smoothness, then whiz in the Tabasco and lemon juice. Lastly, briefly whiz in the chopped parsley – just enough to mix it into the pâté without pulverizing it too much. Scrape the contents of the food processor into a serving bowl, cover and store it in the fridge. Take it into room temperature for 25–30 minutes before serving, to take the fridge chill off the pâté.

Taramasalata

How I do love this simple, rich pâté made from smoked cod's roe and olive oil. But black olives must accompany it, and for me these must be Kalamata olives. Warm toasted granary bread makes this such a treat for a first course, or, with a mixed-leaf salad, as a main course for lunch or supper any time of the year, if you can get hold of smoked cod's roe. It is obtainable in jars out-side its season in February.

Serves 6

225 g/8 oz jar of smoked cod's roe
3 slices of white bread, from a baked loaf not
a steamed one, soaked in cold water
2 garlic cloves, skinned and chopped
300 ml/½ pint extra-virgin olive oil
juice of 2 lemons – about 4 tbsps
lots of black pepper (absolutely no salt:
the roe is salty enough even for me)

Put the contents of the jar into a food processor. Squeeze the water from the bread and put the bread into the processor with the garlic. Whiz, adding the olive oil as if you were making mayonnaise – i.e. in a very thin, steady trickle. When all the olive oil is incorporated, whiz in the lemon juice and season with black pepper. If the mixture is very stiff, whiz in a couple of tablespoons of cold water – it should be the texture of whipped cream. Scoop and scrape the taramasalata into a bowl, cover and store in the fridge until 30 minutes before serving with Kalamata olives and hot granary toast.

Sardine and mushroom pâté

This is an old favourite of mine which belongs in any book on fish! It is strange to me that Godfrey, who so vociferously dislikes sardines (I love them), loves this pâté – illogical, isn't it? The sardines in this recipe are tinned: we can now buy good sardines preserved in olive oil, which taste so much better. Sardines, including tinned ones, are rich in omega-3 oils and therefore we should eat them regularly – no hardship! This pâté, by the way, makes a very good filling for buns for a picnic.

Serves 6

450 g/1 lb mushrooms, wiped and chopped
3 tbsps olive oil
½ tsp flaky salt (Maldon, ideally)
2 tins of sardines preserved in olive oil
375 g/12 oz cream cheese, such as Philadelphia
lots of black pepper
2 tbsps lemon juice
1 tbsp chopped parsley

Start by cooking the mushrooms. Mix them with the olive oil, then either fry them in a sauté pan over a high heat, or line a baking tray with baking parchment (makes washing up so much easier) and put them on to this. Scatter the salt over the mushrooms and roast them in a hot oven, 220°C/450°F/gas mark 7 (top-right oven in a four-door Aga), for 30 minutes. They should be very well roasted to maximize their flavour – a tip given to me by my late and much-missed great friend and gourmet Brigadier Hugh Ley. Cool the roast or fried mushrooms.

first courses or savouries, lunch or supper dishes

Drain the sardines well – I do this by opening the tins in the sink and carefully pouring off the oil down the plughole; this saves getting fish oil on the work surface. Put the drained sardines into a food processor. Add the cooled mushrooms and whiz, adding the cream cheese, black pepper, lemon juice and, finally, the chopped parsley. Scrape the contents of the processor into a bowl to serve.

This can be made a day ahead and kept in a covered bowl in the fridge till 30 minutes before serving. I like to serve it with toasted granary bread.

Flaked smoked mackerel and apple and chive pâté

This is a very different version of smoked mackerel pâté. It is textured, with the fish left in juicy flakes, and the apples and horseradish add good contrasting textures and complementary tastes to the fish. Any version of a dish using smoked mackerel encourages us to make the most of this simple but delicious fish which, with its omega-3 oils, is so full of goodness.

Serves 6

3 smoked mackerel fillets
3 good eating apples
375 g/12 oz cream cheese (Philadelphia Lite will
    give a softer texture than full-fat)
2 tsps best-quality creamy horseradish sauce, preferably
    Moniack or Isabella Massie
3 tbsps lemon juice
lots of black pepper (no need for salt: the fish adds enough saltiness)
2 tbsps snipped chives

Flake the smoked mackerel into a bowl, carefully removing any bones or skin. Peel, core and neatly chop the apples into thumbnail-sized bits.

In a bowl, beat the cream cheese till softer, adding the horseradish, lemon juice, black pepper and chives. You need the cream cheese soft enough so that you can mix in the chopped apples and the flaked smoked mackerel fairly easily, without breaking up either the fish or the apples more than you can help. When all is mixed together, heap the pâté into a serving bowl.

This rather more rustic pâté is good with warm brown or granary bread torn in chunks, and, if you like, with salad leaves dressed with a Dijon mustard vinaigrette.

Prawn, bacon and cream cheese pâté

I repeat this, with a couple of alterations, from an earlier book, and I do so because this is one of the recipes which I am told repeatedly is the prop and mainstay for so many of my cookbook users. Therefore, it belongs in this book on fish. I would say that, if you can, you should use langoustines as the prawn content, because they are by far the most succulent and sweet of all types of prawn. The only prawns I beg you not to use are the tiny pink things which can only be bought frozen. On thawing they taste of soggy blotting paper! Again, here we find the surprisingly delicious combination of bacon with shellfish. This is such an easy pâté and yet it tastes so good. It can be used as a first course, but it is also an excellent sandwich filler for special occasion picnics. I think it is best with granary bread.

Serves 6

450 g/1 lb cream cheese (you can use a reduced-fat
type such as Philadelphia Lite,
but the pâté will have a softer texture
1 fat garlic clove, skinned and chopped finely
1 tbsp lemon juice
110 g/4 oz fresh prawns, chopped
8 rashers of smoked streaky bacon, grilled until
crisp, then broken into bits
a pinch of salt
lots of black pepper
2 tbsps chopped parsley

Whiz the cream cheese in a food processor with the garlic and lemon juice till smooth. Scrape this into a bowl and mix in the chopped prawns, crispy bits of bacon, salt, black pepper and chopped parsley;

Prawn, bacon and cream cheese pâté

don't be tempted to add these to the processor, because if they whiz into the cream cheese one of the attractions of this pâté is lost – its texture contrasts. So mix the chopped prawns and bacon bits in well, but by hand. Pile this mixture into a serving bowl ready to serve – no need for further garnish. It can be made several hours in advance, but it is best eaten the day it is made. Serve with brown toast or Melba toast.

Potted crab

I was born and spent part of my growing-up years near Morecambe Bay, where the shrimps come from. These tiny, slightly peppery-tasting crustacea are delicious potted, for which they are tossed in melted butter flavoured with mace, then packed in small pots and sealed with melted butter. But for potted crab, melted butter to bind the crabmeat is altogether too rich – crab is so very rich a shellfish already. Instead I use a small amount of mayonnaise. It is, I hope you will agree, an utterly delicious way to eat crab.

Serves 6

For the mayonnaise

1 whole egg
1 egg yolk
1 level tsp caster sugar
½ tsp salt
plenty of ground black pepper
1 level tsp mustard powder
2 tsps Tabasco
150 ml/¼ pint olive oil
juice of 1 lemon

675 g/1½ lb crabmeat, equal quantities of white and brown mixed well
2 tbsps mayonnaise (see above)
6 sprigs dill
175 g/6 oz butter, melted

Make the mayonnaise by putting the egg and egg yolk, sugar, salt, pepper, mustard powder and Tabasco into a processor and, whizzing, gradually adding the olive oil. When you have a thick emulsion, add the lemon juice. Mix the crabmeat into 2 tablespoons of the mayonnaise, and divide evenly between six ramekins. Smooth, and put a small sprig of dill on each. Carefully pour melted butter over the surface of each ramekin, and put the ramekins into the fridge till you are ready to serve them. I like this best served with Melba toast, which can be made a day in advance and kept in a sealed polythene bag or airtight container.

Devilled herring roes on toast

Getting hold of soft herring roes is not easy, but ask a fish merchant and they can be procured. For those of us who love them they are a treat bordering on a delicacy!

Serves 6

2 tbsps sieved flour
½ tsp salt
plenty of black pepper, ground fine
a dusting of cayenne pepper (a pinch would be
    my measurement, but I do not advise pinching
    cayenne pepper: its ferocity lingers on the
    fingers for hours)
900 g/2 lb soft herring roes
75 g/3 oz butter and 1 tbsp olive oil
6 thick slices of granary (or white, if you prefer) bread
1 lemon cut into 6 wedges

Put the flour, salt, pepper and cayenne into a large polythene bag. Add the herring roes and immediately shake the bag vigorously, to coat each roe with seasoned flour. Tip the contents on to a large dish.

Heat the butter and olive oil together in a wide sauté pan till hot and foaming. Fry the coated herring roes – they will curl up as they cook. Turn each over and cook for about 1 minute in total. Meanwhile, toast and butter the bread, then lift the cooked herring roes on to the buttered slices of toast, one piece of toast on each of six warmed plates. Serve immediately, with a piece of lemon on each plate.

first courses or savouries, lunch or supper dishes

Cod roe with apple slices and bacon

This is just as good for a breakfast, lunch or supper dish as for a first course. It is a thoroughly adaptable dish, with everything you need on one plate. The apple slices can have their skins left on or not, as you prefer – I leave mine on. The season for cod roe is so short – February – that this dish is worth eating at any hour of the twenty-four if you love cod roe. Godfrey loves it; I would much prefer herring roes. Bacon has such a great taste affinity with all types of fish and shellfish, and the roe of fish, in this case cod, is no exception.

2 rashers of best-quality (dry-cured) back bacon per person, smoked or unsmoked, as you prefer

olive oil

1 slice of cod roe per person, about 1 cm/½ inch thick

2 slices of eating apple per person

a dash of Tabasco

black pepper

Grill the bacon rashers to the degree of done-ness that you like.

For the cod roe, for preference, use a non-stick sauté pan. Heat the merest smear of olive oil in the pan and, when it is hot, fry the slices of cod roe. When you put them in the pan leave them alone – do not be tempted to shove them around the pan surface with your fish slice. After about 1 minute carefully turn over each slice to cook on its other side. They should be crisp on the surface. As they cook, fry the slices of apple at the same time. (Depending how many you are cooking for, you may not have room in the sauté pan for both cod roe and apple slices at the same time, in which case fry the apple slices first and keep them warm on a plate while you fry the cod roe slices.) Cook the apple till each slice is just tender when stuck with a fork. Add the Tabasco and season with black pepper.

Serve a slice of cod roe, two bacon rashers and two slices of apple on each warmed plate.

Potted shrimps

This takes me back to my childhood. My father was in the Royal Navy and we lived, for the most part, 15 miles from Morecambe Bay. Potted shrimps were what my mother always made for a big 'do'. Bought potted shrimps aren't a patch on home-made ones. It all depends on quality – the tiny brownish shrimps only really come from the north-west, Morecambe Bay being a part of this area. Almost as important is the butter used – and this is where bought, frozen potted shrimps fall down: they use inferior butter in their making! I use Lurpak lightly salted butter. Mace is imperative as a seasoning – the outer husk of the nutmeg, mace has great affinity with shrimps, and with all other fish too.

Serves 6

225 g/8 oz Lurpak butter
2 blades of mace
lots of finely ground black pepper
575 g/1¼ lb shrimps, weighed when shelled

Start with the butter, which must be clarified. This is easy: just put the butter into a saucepan with the blades of mace, on the lowest possible heat. If you cook on an Aga, just put the saucepan with the butter on the back of the Aga and leave it until the butter has very slowly melted. As it warms through, the mace will infuse the butter with its flavour. Season the butter, too, with lots of finely ground black pepper.

Divide the shrimps between six ramekins. Very carefully pour the butter from the pan over the shrimps, leaving the white milky bit at the bottom of the pan – it is the clear oil which is the clarified butter. Remove the blades of mace. Leave each ramekin until the butter covering the shrimps has set, then carefully cover each ramekin with clingfilm and store them in the fridge till you are ready to serve them. They are good with toasted granary bread and a wedge of lemon beside each ramekin.

Marinated salmon and smoked salmon in lime with crème fraîche, pink peppercorns and cucumber

I have done various versions of this recipe over the years, but this is my definite favourite. I love the pink peppercorns with the fish. The success of this dish depends entirely on the quality of the salmon used: we use organically farmed fresh salmon. The diced cucumber must be from cucumber which is de-seeded first, otherwise the seeds will seep liquid and dilute the dressing, which spoils the whole thing. This dish makes an ideal first course because it can be done a day in advance. It is also a delicious main course for lunch or supper on a hot summer day. This amount will serve 4 as a main course.

Serves 6

450 g/1 lb organically farmed or wild salmon, skin
and bone removed, and sliced into neat dice,
about thumbnail-size
rind and juice of 4 limes, *or* 2 lemons instead, well
washed to remove preservative and dried
before grating
½ cucumber, peeled, halved lengthways and seeded
450 g/1 lb best-quality smoked salmon, diced thumbnail-size
450 ml/¾ pint crème fraîche
2 tsps pink peppercorns, drained of their brine
1 tbsp torn dillweed
black pepper

Put the diced fresh salmon into a wide dish and add the lime rinds and juice. Mix thoroughly, cover the dish with clingfilm and leave for 3–4 hours minimum, or overnight. Try to mix the diced salmon

Marinated salmon and smoked salmon in lime with créme fraîche, pink peppercorns and cucumber

around in the marinade once or twice during the hours it sits, and store it in the fridge. The fish will become opaque in colour – it literally cooks in the acid lime juice.

Cut the seeded cucumber into neat, fine dice and put these into a mixing bowl. Add the diced smoked salmon, the crème fraîche, pink peppercorns and torn dill. When the fresh salmon has marinated for several hours, drain off the lime juices and mix the fish into the contents of the bowl. Season with black pepper and serve, heaped on a white dish and accompanied by warm bread or Melba toast.

first courses or savouries, lunch or supper dishes

Avruga and crème fraîche with smoked salmon

Surely one of the easiest of first courses, but these tastes go together so well. Avruga is grainy herring roe (as opposed to the soft roes) preserved with just a squeeze of lemon juice. It is bought in glass jars and is utterly delicious. It isn't trying to be a poor man's caviar, like the awful lumpfish roe, and personally I like it better than the finest oscietra caviar. Mixed into crème fraîche it just tastes so good with smoked salmon. This is hardly a recipe, more a combination of ingredients, but it is so good that we had this for the first course at our daughter Isabella and son-in-law Tom's wedding!

Serves 6

300 ml/½ pint crème fraîche
6 tbsps avruga
a good grinding of black pepper – no need for any salt
12 slices of the best-quality smoked salmon
finely chopped parsley – about a tablespoonful
1 lemon, cut in half, then each half cut into 3 wedges

In a bowl, carefully – so as not to crush the tiny eggs of the roes – mix together the crème fraîche and avruga, seasoning with black pepper. You can do this a day in advance if it is more convenient for you, but cover the bowl with clingfilm and leave it in the fridge till you are ready to assemble the first course.

On each of six plates lay 2 slices of smoked salmon. Using two dessertspoons, scoop quenelle shapes of the avruga mixture at one side of the smoked salmon slices. Scatter a small amount of chopped parsley over the avruga mixture on each serving and put a lemon wedge at the side of each.

Smoked salmon with toasted pecan bread roulades

These brown bread rolls with their butter and crunchy pecan filling just dress up smoked salmon. They are delicious. The lemon in the butter goes well with the smoked salmon, and the toasted pecans give a good contrasting crunch. They can be made several hours in advance if they are covered with clingfilm till just before serving.

Serves 6

110 g/4 oz pecans
225 g/8 oz soft butter
finely grated rind of 1 lemon, well washed and dried before grating
½ tsp flaky salt
lots of black pepper
12 slices of brown bread (I prefer granary)
12 slices of smoked salmon
1 lemon, each half cut into 3 wedges

Roast the pecans, or dry-fry them in a sauté pan until crisp. Cool them, then bash them (I use a rolling pin) to break them up. Put the butter into a bowl and beat it with the grated lemon rind, salt, black pepper and, lastly, the broken nuts. Mix all very well together.

With a sharp serrated knife cut the crusts off the slices of bread and with a rolling pin roll each slice. Divide the butter mixture between the 12 slices of crustless, rolled and flattened bread, spreading it evenly over each slice. Then roll up each slice tightly, and cut it in half.

Put two slices of smoked salmon on each of the six plates. Either put the pecan bread roulades at the side of the smoked salmon, two per plate, or pile the roulades on to a plate and hand them separately. Put a lemon wedge at the side of each plate.

first courses or savouries, lunch or supper dishes

Carpaccio of tuna with cracked black pepper and grape and lime salsa

This is easy to assemble and convenient to make. The grape and lime salsa can be put together a day in advance, but it should be kept in a covered bowl in the fridge. The tuna must be sliced wafer thin – ask the fish merchant to do this for you, or you can do it yourself if you slice the tuna in a mandolin or, better still, if you own a slicer. This recipe makes such a light but delicious first course.

Serves 6

5 wafer-thin slices of tuna per person (i.e. 30 slices of tuna)
approx. 3 tsps cracked black pepper
extra-virgin olive oil

450 g/1 lb sweet seedless grapes, preferably red or black, *For the salsa*
washed, dried and cut in quarters
2 tbsps snipped chives
2 sticks celery, well washed, trimmed and sliced as
thinly as possible
juice and finely grated rind of 2 limes, well washed to
remove preservative and dried before grating
3 tbsps olive oil
½ tsp salt

On each of six plates arrange 5 slices of tuna in a circle, slightly over-lapping the slices. Scatter the cracked black pepper over the tuna. (Some peppermills grind sufficiently coarsely to produce cracked black pepper; otherwise, use a pestle and mortar or a deep bowl and the end of a rolling pin, and do the pounding with the bowl in your sink. This helps prevent peppercorns from jumping out of the bowl

Carpaccio of tuna with cracked black pepper and grape and lime salsa

and scooting all around the kitchen.) Trickle a thin stream of olive oil over the tuna slices.

Make the salsa by stirring all the ingredients together in a bowl, mixing thoroughly. Divide the salsa between the six plates, putting a small heap in the centre of the tuna slices. You can assemble this dish several hours ahead of serving, but loosely cover the plates with clingfilm and keep them in a cool place until you are ready to uncover them and put them around the table.

Squid with garlic and parsley

I love to use squid when we can get it. Squid, like sea bass, prefer warmer waters, so our supplies are only really plentiful in middle to late summer. Squid are nicest when they are simply cooked, as in this recipe. It is impera-tive to remove the skin completely. Any thin membrane left on will be tough to eat. Squid is no different from other seafood – it is ruined by overcooking, and will become rubbery of texture if sautéed for too long. Serve the squid warm or cold, whichever the weather dictates or you prefer.

Serves 6

900 g/2 lb squid, weighed when trimmed
6 tbsps extra-virgin olive oil
2 cloves garlic, skinned and finely chopped
½ tsp flaky salt, preferably Maldon
a good grinding of black pepper
1 red chilli, seeded and finely chopped (optional)
2 good handfuls of parsley, flat-leaved if at all possible, chopped

Prepare the squid by gently pulling the plastic-like end of the quill – you will find this sticking out a little bit at the base of the body. When you gently pull, the entrails should come out with the quill. Wash out the inside of the squid under running cold water. Peel off the mottled skin and inner membrane. Slice the squid in rings, each about 0.5 cm/¼ inch thick. Cut the tentacles into lengths of about 1.5 cms/ ¾ inch. You can do this preparation several hours before cooking, but cover the bowl of squid and keep it in the fridge.

To cook, heat the olive oil in a large sauté pan and add the squid and the garlic. Over a fairly high heat, stir everything around in the pan until the squid is opaque. Season with salt and pepper (and chilli, if you are using it), then stir in the parsley just before serving. If served cold, the squid benefits from a further trickle of olive oil and a squeeze of lemon, neither of which you need if it is served warm.

Oysters stir-fried with ginger and spring onions

This is a first course which takes seconds to cook. Much as I do loathe raw oysters, I love them cooked, with their silky texture. Their size determines how many oysters per person, but I reckon between five and six.

Serves 6

4 tbsps olive oil
about 4 cm/2 inches fresh ginger, skin pared off
    and the ginger grated finely
about 30 spring onions, tatty outer leaves and
    end of bulb removed, the spring onions
    sliced into thin strips
½ tsp chopped fresh chilli (optional)
30 oysters, removed from their shells
black pepper
¼ tsp salt

Heat the olive oil in a sauté pan and stir-fry the chopped ginger and spring onions, and the chilli if you are using it, over a high heat for a minute. This should be enough to wilt the spring onions and to take the ferocity off the raw ginger. Then add the shelled oysters to the pan and stir-fry all together, just until the oysters turn opaque and firm – about another minute. Season with black pepper and salt, then serve. This won't hurt if it is kept warm – it is good served warm rather than hot straight from the stove, just beware drying out the plump oysters.

first courses or savouries, lunch or supper dishes

Prawn cocktail

*Very much a first course from the 1960s and synonymous with the era of
Black Forest gâteau, prawn cocktail seems to be making a comeback. If you
can banish all thoughts of harsh, vinegary, bright pink, bottled Sauce Marie
Rose from your mind, a prawn cocktail can be a most delicious treat. If you
can, get langoustines and chop them if they are very large. If you can't get
langoustines, use any good-quality type of prawn (see Introduction, page 21)
but avoid those small frozen pink things which taste of wet cardboard when
thawed and which, I suspect, owe nothing to nature but must somehow be
produced in a factory. Adjust the amounts of flavouring ingredients in the
sauce according to your taste, but below is how I like it. And use any lettuce
except that 1960s leaf, the iceberg!*

Serves 6

300 ml/½ pint double cream   *For the sauce*
2 tbsps Worcester sauce
1 tbsp lemon juice
2 tsps tomato purée
a shake of Tabasco
1 tsp Dijon mustard
3 tbsps mayonnaise – home-made,
if at all possible (see page 250)
a good grinding of black pepper
½ tsp salt

450 g/1 lb prawns, weighed when shelled, cut in half
if they are very large
assorted lettuce leaves
a dusting of cayenne pepper, to garnish
6 lemon wedges, to garnish

Prawn cocktail

Add the Worcester sauce, lemon juice, tomato purée, Tabasco and Dijon mustard to the cream and whip (not too stiffly). Fold in the mayonnaise. Taste, and add salt and pepper accordingly. Fold the prawns into the sauce . You can do this in the morning, cover the bowl and leave it in the fridge till you are ready to assemble the cocktails.

Divide the leaves (tear them up if they are large) between six large glass goblets. Divide the prawns in their sauce, spooning them over the leaves. A dust of cayenne pepper or a wedge of lemon at the side of each glass is needed by way of a garnish. Serve with Melba toast.

Sardines on chilli and lemon-buttered toast

This is the perfect supper for a Sunday evening, but of course it can be eaten at any time on any day! Served in smaller quantities, it makes a good savoury for four people.

Serves 2

¼ tsp chilli flakes
finely grated rind of 1 lemon, well washed
to remove preservative
and dried before grating
75 g/3 oz soft butter
2 tins of sardines, preserved in olive oil
black pepper
2 slices of thick granary bread
(or white, if you prefer)

In a bowl, work the chilli flakes and grated lemon rind into the soft butter, mixing well.

Drain the sardines by opening the tins over the sink and carefully pouring off the oil down the plughole. Tip the sardines into a bowl, season them with black pepper and, with a fork, mash them till they are almost smooth.

Toast the bread. Spread the butter on the hot toast and heap the mashed sardines on top, dividing them equally between the slices. Eat immediately.

Crab mayonnaise on avocado mousse

This makes a very good first course, but it can also be a main course for lunch or supper in the summer months (in which case it will serve 4). The crab must be of the finest quality, and the mayonnaise should be home-made – there just doesn't exist a commercial mayonnaise that can touch home-made. I have tried so many bought mayonnaises: some are positively revolting and the best is mildly disappointing. So we must continue to make our own!

I like to serve this mousse in a glass bowl, because the two-colour layers look attractive seen through glass.

Serves 6

450 g/1 lb best-quality crabmeat, equal quantities of white and brown meats
1 heaped tbsp chopped parsley and snipped chives, mixed

For the mayonnaise
1 egg
1 egg yolk
1 rounded tsp Dijon mustard
½ tsp salt
1 tsp caster sugar
a good grinding of black pepper
300 ml/½ pint light olive oil
2 tbsps lemon juice
1 tsp white wine vinegar

For the avocado mousse
300 ml/½ pint chicken stock
3 leaves of gelatine, soaked in cold water
3 avocados, preferably of the dark, knobbly-skinned type
3 tbsps lemon juice
a good dash of Tabasco
½ tsp salt
lots of black pepper
300 ml/½ pint crème fraîche
2 egg whites and a pinch of salt

To make the mayonnaise, put the egg, yolk, mustard, salt, sugar and pepper into a food processor and whiz. Gradually add the olive oil, drop by drop initially and then, when you safely have an emulsion, in a thin, steady trickle till all the oil is incorporated. Whiz in the lemon juice and white wine vinegar. Taste, and add more of anything if you think it is needed – you may like a sharper taste, in which case add more wine vinegar, by the teaspoonful. Scrape the contents of the food processor into a bowl and stir in the chopped parsley and chives, and crabmeats, mixing all together well. Put the bowl, covered, into the fridge.

To make the avocado mousse, heat the stock and, when it is hot, drop in the soaked gelatine leaves. Swirl the contents of the saucepan until the gelatine dissolves, which will be almost instantly. Leave to get cold and start to gel.

Cut each avocado in half and flick out the stones with the point of a knife. With a spoon, scoop out the flesh, scraping inside the skins to get the most of the deeper colour which lies just inside the skins. Put the avocado flesh into a food processor. Add the lemon juice and whiz, gradually adding the gelling stock and the Tabasco. Whiz in the salt and pepper, then, briefly, whiz in the crème fraîche.

In a bowl, whisk the 2 egg whites and the pinch of salt till stiff (the salt gives increased volume as the whites whisk up). With either a large metal spoon or a batter whisk, fold some of the whisked whites into the avocado mixture. Then scrape the contents of the processor into the egg-white bowl (I know one shouldn't, but it really doesn't make any difference and it does save washing up an unnecessary bowl!) and fold the two mixtures together thoroughly. Pour this into a glass bowl (preferably uncut glass), cover the bowl and leave the mousse to set. When it is set, spoon the crab mayonnaise over the entire surface. Serve with Melba toast or warmed bread.

Crab mousse

This makes a very good first course, but it is also an excellent main course, accompanied by a mixed-leaf salad, for lunch or supper in hot weather. It is simple and delicious, because it uses both white and brown crabmeats – the white has such a good texture but the brown meat has much more flavour. Buy the very best crab you can. This amount will serve four as a main course.

Serves 6

300 ml/½ pint fish or vegetable stock
4 leaves of gelatine, soaked in cold water
450 g/1 lb crabmeat, equal quantities of white and brown
2 tbsps lemon juice
a good dash of Tabasco
½ tsp salt
a good grinding of black pepper
300 ml/½ pint crème fraîche
2 egg whites and a pinch of salt
dill, to garnish (optional)

Warm the stock and drop the soaked gelatine leaves into it. Swirl the saucepan until the gelatine has dissolved completely, then set the pan on one side to let the liquid cool and just begin to gel.

Mix the crabmeats together well, adding the lemon juice and Tabasco, salt and pepper. Mix in the cold, gelling stock. Fold in the crème fraîche. Lastly, whisk up the egg whites with the pinch of salt (the salt gives increased volume as the whites whisk up) until the whites are stiff. Fold them quickly and thoroughly through the crab mixture, and pour this into a dish to set. Cover the dish with clingfilm and leave in the fridge until required. Put a generous frond of dill on the surface of the mousse, if you like, as a garnish.

Serve with Melba toast – the crispness contrasts with the creamy-textured mousse.

Hot-smoked salmon and avocado terrine

This is delicious, but fairly filling if eaten in quantity. It is suitable for a first course, or for a lunch or supper main course in hot weather, accompanied by a mixed-leaf salad. I like to use a Pyrex terrine-shaped dish to set it in – these are quite widely available and good for anything containing avocado, because I find that metal loaf tins, even when lined with clingfilm, cause the avocado to discolour.

Serves 6–8

450 ml/¾ pint chicken or vegetable stock
6 leaves of gelatine, soaked in cold water for 10 minutes
450 g/1 lb hot-smoked salmon, flaked from the skin
2 tbsps chopped parsley and snipped chives, mixed
½ tsp salt
a good grinding of black pepper
4 avocados, preferably the dark, knobbly-skinned variety,
or 3 of the larger, paler, smooth-skinned type
2 tbsps lemon juice
a dash of Tabasco
450 ml/¾ pint crème fraîche

Line a 1.8-litre/3-pint Pyrex terrine dish with clingfilm, carefully pushing it right into each corner. A small wedge of screwed-up kitchen paper is good for this, otherwise it can be too easy to push your finger through the clingfilm.

Heat the stock and, when it is warm – not anywhere near boiling – drop in the soaked leaves of gelatine and swirl the saucepan a couple of times to dissolve the gelatine. Cool, then pour half this amount into a bowl with the flaked hot-smoked salmon. Stir in the chopped parsley and snipped chives and season with salt and pepper.

Hot-smoked salmon and avocado terrine

Scoop the flesh of the avocados from the skin, scraping right inside the skins to get the maximum green colour, and put the flesh into a food processor. Whiz, adding the lemon juice, Tabasco and the remainder of the gelling stock. Lastly, briefly whiz in the crème fraîche. Scrape half this mixture from the processor into the cling-film-lined Pyrex dish. Leave until *just* set. Then fork over the flaked salmon and herbs, and scrape the rest of the avocado mixture on top. Carefully bang the dish on the work surface a couple of times to dislodge any small air pockets, cover the dish and leave to set for several hours – I make this in the morning for eating that evening.

To turn out, remove the surface clingfilm. Invert the dish on to a serving plate and lift off the Pyrex dish. Carefully peel off the clingfilm which lined the terrine dish and which will be clinging to the terrine itself. Surround the terrine with salad leaves or with clumps of watercress, and slice thickly to serve. The colour contrast between the smooth, pale green avocado mixture and the pink of the hot-smoked salmon, and the texture contrast too between the smoothness and the flaked fish, is very satisfying I find. And it tastes good!

Smoked trout and horseradish mousse

This is such a favourite of mine, using hot-smoked trout fillets. The combined taste of smoked trout and horseradish is excellent, but the horseradish must be creamy and not harshly vinegary as in the mass-produced commercial horseradish sauces. The best, I think, is that made by Isabella Massie in Aberdeenshire. This is a convenient first course as well as a delicious one, because the mousse can be made a day in advance and kept in a covered bowl in the fridge till half an hour before serving.

Serves 6

150 ml/¼ pint single cream
3 leaves of gelatine, soaked in cold water
4 smoked trout fillets – total weight about 450 g/1 lb
2 tbsps lemon juice
2 rounded tsps creamy horseradish sauce
lots of black pepper
300 ml/½ pint crème fraîche
2 egg whites and a pinch of salt

Put the single cream into a saucepan and heat. Drop the soaked gelatine leaves into the warmed cream and swirl the pan to dissolve the gelatine in the heat of the cream.

Put the smoked trout fillets into a food processor, removing any bones you encounter. Add the lemon juice and horseradish to the trout, and whiz, adding the gelatine cream. Season with black

Smoked trout and horseradish mousse

pepper, and add the crème fraîche, whizzing it in very briefly so as not to curdle it. Whisk the egg whites and pinch of salt in a bowl until they are stiff. Fold a small amount of whisked whites through the smoked trout mixture in the processor bowl, then scrape this into the bowl containing the whisked whites and fold both together thoroughly. Scrape the mousse into a serving bowl, cover with clingfilm and keep the bowl in the fridge till half an hour before serving. Serve with the Horseradish, Apple and Crème Fraîche Dressing on page 256 if you like. And Melba toast is good with this.

Shrimp, spinach and bacon roulade

This can be a first course, or it can, in larger amounts per person, be a very good main course. The taste combination of the shrimps with the bacon and spinach is a very good one. I use frozen leaf spinach in this recipe because I find it easier to work with in a roulade. This need only be accompanied by a mixed-leaf salad, and perhaps new potatoes in season, or warm bread or rolls if it is destined to be a main course. As a first course, it really needs no accompaniment other than vinaigrette-dressed salad leaves.

Serves 6–8

900 g/2 lb frozen leaf spinach, thawed *For the roulade*
and excess water squeezed from it
50 g/2 oz butter
50 g/2 oz grated Parmesan cheese
4 large eggs, yolks separated from whites
½ teaspoon salt
lots of black pepper
a good grating of nutmeg

50 g/2 oz butter *For the sauce to*
1 rounded tbsp flour *fill the cooked*
600 ml/1 pint milk *roulade*
½ teaspoon salt
lots of black pepper
a grating of nutmeg
450 g/1 lb shrimps, weighed when shelled; buy them fresh,
not frozen, if at all possible
4 rashers of back smoked or unsmoked bacon, grilled, trimmed
of fat and cut into slivers – I use scissors
2 tbsps chopped parsley and snipped chives, mixed

Shrimp, spinach and bacon roulade

Line a baking tray with a large piece of baking parchment – the tin should measure about 30 x 35 cm/12 x 14 inches. Stick the parchment into each corner with a small piece of butter.

Start by making the roulade. Put the spinach into a food processor and whiz, adding the butter, Parmesan cheese and egg yolks, one at a time. Season with salt, pepper and nutmeg.

In a large bowl add a pinch of salt to the egg whites (this gives increased volume) and whisk the whites till stiff. Fold some of the whisked whites into the spinach mixture, then scrape the spinach mixture into the rest of the egg whites. This saves washing up another bowl and, although it is a bit tricky folding the whites into the spinach in the food processor bowl, it can be done. Fold the spinach and egg whites together thoroughly. Pour and scrape this mixture over the parchment-lined baking tray, pushing it into the corners and smoothing it even. Bake in a moderate heat, 180°C/350°F/gas mark 4 (bottom-right oven in a four-door Aga), for 20–30 minutes, or until it is firm to touch when lightly pressed.

While the roulade is cooking, make the sauce by melting the butter in a saucepan. Stir in the flour and let this mixture cook for a minute before gradually adding the milk, stirring continuously until the sauce bubbles. Season with salt, pepper and nutmeg, take the pan off the heat and stir in the shrimps and cooked bacon slivers. Stir in the chopped parsley and snipped chives.

When the roulade is cooked, take it from the oven, put a clean sheet of baking parchment on to a work surface and tip the cooked roulade face down, as it were, on to the paper. Carefully tear the baking parchment from the back of the roulade, tearing in strips along the roulade, to prevent tugging the roulade with the paper. Spread the shrimp and bacon sauce over the surface, and roll up the roulade into a long roll, slipping it from the paper on to a warm serving plate. Serve as soon as possible, sliced on to warmed plates. This will keep warm, but not for much longer than 15 minutes. If you want to keep it warm, put a sheet of foil loosely over it to hold in the heat.

first courses or savouries, lunch or supper dishes

Smoked haddock, lime and parsley mousse

This has a hint of chilli in the ingredients. When I look back over my many versions of smoked haddock mousse, they vary enormously. Twenty-five years ago I used a white sauce base – times change, and this is what we make these days at Kinloch, and we think it is the best of all smoked haddock mousses. It really goes without saying that the smoked haddock should be pale-coloured and plump, and absolutely not dyed hideous, vivid yellow.

This mousse, in larger quantities per person, makes a very good lunch or supper main course in warm weather, with a mixed-leaf salad to go with it, and warm bread or rolls, or new potatoes in season. But here it is meant for use as a first course.

Serves 6

450 g/1 lb plump smoked haddock fillets, all skin and
bones removed
milk to cover the fish in its dish
scant ½ tsp dried chilli flakes
4 leaves of gelatine, soaked in cold water
450 ml/¾ pint crème fraîche
finely grated rind of 2 limes, washed well to remove
preservative and dried before grating
2 tbsps chopped parsley
lots of black pepper (no salt: the fish will contribute enough)
2 egg whites and a pinch of salt

Put the fish into an ovenproof dish and cover with the milk. Bake it in a moderate oven, 180°/350°F/gas mark 4 (bottom-right oven in a four-door Aga), for 20 minutes, then allow the fish to cool in the milk. Alternatively, cook the fish in the milk in a saucepan on top of the cooker, heating till the milk just simmers, then simmer for 1 minute before taking the pan off the heat and letting the fish cool in the milk. Whichever way you have cooked it, strain 300 ml/½ pint of the milk into a saucepan, add the chilli flakes, and warm it through. Drop the

Smoked haddock, lime and parsley mousse

soaked gelatine leaves into this warm milk and swirl the pan to dissolve the gelatine in the heat of the milk.

Flake the cooked fish into a bowl. Mix in the gelatine milk, and leave to grow cold and start to gel. When just beginning to gel, mix in the crème fraîche, lime rinds and parsley, and season with black pepper. In a large bowl, whisk up the egg whites and the pinch of salt till the whites are stiff. With a large metal spoon or a flat whisk, fold the whisked whites through the smoked haddock and parsley mixture. Pour and scrape this into a serving dish, cover the dish with clingfilm, and keep it in the fridge till half an hour before serving. This mousse looks pretty and has a contrast of texture with the juicy flaked smoked haddock. I like to serve it with Melba toast.

first courses or savouries, lunch or supper dishes

Watercress roulade with smoked salmon

This is such a good first course, but it can also be a main course in the summer, for lunch or dinner. And it can form the main part of a more elegant picnic, for those occasions when knife-and-fork picnic food is called for, because it is easily transported, easy to slice and serve, very good to eat and it looks pretty.

Serves 6–8

600 ml/1 pint milk	*For the flavoured milk*
1 onion, skinned and halved	
a stick of celery, washed and halved	
a frond of fennel (optional)	
a few black peppercorns	
1 tsp rock salt	
a handful of parsley	
50 g/2 oz butter	*For the roulade*
50 g/2 oz flour	
2 handfuls of watercress	
salt	
freshly ground black pepper	
1 egg	
4 large eggs, separated	
grated rind and juice of 1 lemon, washed well to remove preservative and dried before grating	*For the filling*
450 ml/¾ pint double cream, whipped	
plenty of freshly ground black pepper	
225 g/8 oz smoked salmon, cut into fairly fine shreds	

Watercress roulade with smoked salmon

Bring the milk to scalding point in a saucepan, together with the flavourings. Once the milk has reached scalding point, take the pan off the heat and leave it to stand for an hour, then strain the milk, throwing away the flavourings.

Line a baking tray measuring about 30 x 35 cm/12 x 14 inches with baking parchment. Melt the butter in a saucepan, stir in the flour and let it cook for a couple of minutes to make a roux. Liquidize the watercress with the flavoured milk and add gradually to the roux, stirring continuously till the sauce boils. Season with salt and pepper, and take the pan off the heat. Beat in the whole egg and 4 egg yolks. Whisk the 4 egg whites till they are very stiff, then, with a large metal spoon, fold them quickly into the sauce. Pour this into the lined baking tray, and bake in a moderate oven, 180°C/350°F/gas mark 4 (bottom-right oven in a four-door Aga), for about 25 minutes, till it feels firm to the touch. Take it out of the oven, cover with a fresh piece of baking parchment and a damp tea towel over that, and leave to cool.

To make the filling, whip the lemon juice and rind into the whipped cream, and season with black pepper. Fold the shredded smoked salmon into the cream.

To roll up the roulade, lay a piece of baking parchment on a table or work surface, uncover the roulade and, taking the short ends of its baking parchment in either hand, flip it over on to the work surface. Carefully peel the paper off its back, in strips along the length of the roulade, which will prevent the roulade tearing with the paper. Cover the surface with the smoked-salmon cream, and roll up. Slip it on to a serving plate and slice it thickly (one less thing do on the picnic site) before loosely wrapping the roulade and its plate in foil. Take a large palette knife or fish slice to lift the roulade from the serving dish to each plate.

first courses or savouries, lunch or supper dishes

Smoked salmon and quails' egg salad with dill dressing

This is a good first course, and the dressing can be made a day in advance. The quails' eggs can be boiled a day ahead, but they are much nicer if they are shelled on the same day they are eaten. Use any salad leaves you choose, but for this I like a mustardy leaf, like mustard cress or mizuna.

Serves 6

12 quails' eggs
6 slices of smoked salmon
assorted salad leaves

75 g/3 oz dill   *For the dressing*
1 tsp caster sugar
½ tsp salt
a good grinding of black pepper
1 tsp Dijon mustard
300 ml/½ pint extra-virgin olive oil
3 tbsps lemon juice

Boil the quails' eggs for 3 minutes, then run them under cold water to cool. Shell them and cut them in half lengthways.

Assemble the salad by arranging as you choose the smoked salmon slices and shelled and halved quails' eggs on each of six plates. I like to put 4 halves of egg in the middle of each plate, and drape the smoked salmon around, then I put the salad leaves around the outside.

Smoked salmon and quails' egg salad
with dill dressing

Make the dressing by putting the dill into a food processor and adding the caster sugar, salt, pepper and Dijon mustard. Whiz, gradually adding the olive oil in a thin, steady trickle. Lastly, whiz in the lemon juice. This will keep for two days in a screw-topped jar in the fridge, but give the covered jar a good shake to mix up the dressing before pouring it in small amounts beside the salad leaves on each plate.

Serve with buttered granary bread, or with warmed brown rolls.

Pinhead oatmeal-coated herrings with grainy mustard and cucumber sauce

Pinhead oatmeal makes the most delicious coating for herring, as well as for any other filleted fish, or chicken, but it needs salt mixed in with the oatmeal to bring out its flavour. If you have any trouble finding pinhead oatmeal in a supermarket, try a health-food shop: they are a very good source of ingredients other than just vitamins and mineral supplements! The mustard sauce is traditional, but I like to add fried diced cucumber, which, with the chopped parsley and snipped chives, makes a really good sauce. Herring have far too brief a season – from about the end of June to the end of August. It is so worthwhile making the most of these delicious fish whilst you can get them. And they are very good for us.

Serves 6

50 g/2 oz butter and 1 tbsp olive oil   *For the sauce*
1 cucumber, peeled (I use a potato peeler), cut lengthways, seeded and diced quite small
1 rounded tbsp flour
600 ml/1 pint milk
2 tsps grainy mustard
finely grated rind of 1 lemon, well washed to remove preservative and dried before grating
a pinch of salt
a good grinding of black pepper

375 g/12 oz pinhead oatmeal
½ tsp salt, preferably Maldon
6 herring, each split and gutted – a fish merchant will do this for you
olive oil for frying the coated herring

Pinhead oatmeal-coated herrings with grainy mustard and cucumber sauce

Start by making the sauce. Melt the butter and heat it together with the olive oil in a fairly wide-based saucepan. Stir the diced and seeded cucumber into the melted butter and oil, and cook, stirring occasionally, over a moderate heat (not too hot), for 4–5 minutes. Then stir in the flour, let it cook for a minute or so before gradually adding the milk, stirring all the time until all the milk is incorporated and the sauce bubbles gently. Stir in the grainy mustard and lemon rind, then season with salt and pepper. Cover the surface of the sauce with a disc of baking parchment wrung out in cold water, to prevent a skin forming. The sauce can be reheated gently over a moderate heat before spooning beside each fried herring.

Put the oatmeal and salt, well mixed, on a large plate. Press each side of each herring into this. Heat olive oil in a sauté pan and fry the coated herrings on each side, until the oatmeal is pale toasted in colour. Lift them out and keep them warm on a large, warmed serving plate. You will have to cook them in relays because space in even the widest sauté pan will not permit six herrings to be cooked at the same time, but fear not, they will come to no harm being kept warm until they are all cooked. Serve, with a spoonful of sauce at the side of each.

first courses or savouries, lunch or supper dishes

Herb crêpes with smoked trout and cucumber

The idea for these crêpes was given to me by Angela Fox, as she then was, who became Angela Pargeter when she had her wedding reception here at Kinloch, many years ago; she is still one of the best cooks I know. The crêpe batter can be made a day in advance, and so can the smoked trout filling. But the crêpes must be made the day they are eaten. They really do not take long to make. They cool almost immediately and they can then be filled all ready for eating several hours in advance – but do loosely cover the dish of filled crêpes with a cloth or clingfilm to prevent the air from staling the crêpes, which then renders them leathery in texture. This makes a very good first course, but, with a more generous number of crêpes per person, it can be a good lunch or supper main course in warm weather.

Serves 6

For the crêpes

2 large eggs
110 g/4 oz plain flour
50 g/1 oz butter, melted
300 ml/½ pint milk
½ tsp salt
a good grinding of black pepper
75 g/3 oz chopped parsley, snipped chives and dill, mixed
dill to garnish (optional)

For the filling

4 smoked trout fillets
1 cucumber, peeled, cut lengthways, seeded and diced neatly and small
450 ml/¾ pint crème fraîche
1 tsp good horseradish, such as Isabella Massie's or Moniack
black pepper (no need for salt: the smoked trout adds enough saltiness)

Herb crêpes with smoked trout and cucumber

Make the batter first – it must stand for at least 30 minutes before being made up into crêpes. Put all the batter ingredients into a blender and whiz till smooth – the herbs fleck the batter and both look and taste good when made up into crêpes – then leave the batter to stand.

To make the crêpes, first give the batter a good stir. Heat a tiny – thumbnail-sized – bit of butter in a hot crêpe pan and, when it is foaming, pour in just enough batter that, when you tip and tilt the pan, the base is covered with a thin, even coating. Cook for a minute or two, until the edges just begin to peel in, then tuck your thumbs under the crêpe and flip it over to cook on its other side for a minute or so. Tip the cooked crêpes on to a large plastic tray to cool; stack them when they are cooled and not before.

For the filling, flake the smoked trout into a bowl, watching out for any bones and carefully removing them. Mix into it the diced cucumber, the crème fraîche, horseradish and pepper, mixing all together thoroughly. Assemble the crêpes by laying them out and dividing the smoked trout mixture evenly between each. Roll up each crêpe into a cigar shape, and put two on each of six plates. Lay a frond of dill, if you like, on each serving.

first courses or savouries, lunch or supper dishes

Smoked haddock timbales with watercress sauce

These make a most delicious, elegant and convenient first course. They look pretty, too, when turned out and surrounded by the pale-green-flecked watercress and lime sauce. The smoked haddock timbale mixture can be made up to a day in advance and kept covered in the fridge. However, take it into room temperature for 30 minutes before dividing it between the buttered ramekins, otherwise the chilled mixture straight from the fridge will take much longer to bake.

Serves 6

675 g/1½ lb smoked haddock *For the timbales*
milk and water, to cover the fish
5 large eggs
300 ml/½ pint single cream
lots of black pepper
a good grating of nutmeg (3 turns)

1 quantity of watercress sauce (see page 272)

Put the smoked haddock on a board and feel it with your fingers. Cut out any bones you feel and remove any skin. Cut the fish into smallish chunks, about 2.5 cm/1 inch. Put the fish into a saucepan and cover with milk and water. Over a moderate heat bring the liquid around the fish to a gentle simmering point, take the pan off the heat and drain off the liquid. Put the fish into a food processor – it will be only partially cooked. Whiz, adding the eggs, one by one, and lastly add the cream, whizzing briefly. Season with pepper and nutmeg. Pour this mixture into a large jug, cover, and put the jug into the fridge.

Smoked haddock timbales with watercress sauce

Butter six ramekins thoroughly – this helps so much with the washing up afterwards, as egg when baked sticks like concrete to an unbuttered surface. Stir up the contents of the jug, then divide it between the buttered ramekins. Put the ramekins into a roasting tin, and pour nearly boiling water around them, to come halfway up the sides of the ramekins. Bake in a moderate oven, 180°C/350°F/gas mark 4 (bottom-right oven in a four-door Aga), for 30 minutes, or until they feel firm when lightly pressed. Take them from the oven and leave them to stand for 10 minutes before turning them out by running a knife around the inside of each ramekin and then shaking each gently on to a warmed serving plate. Pour some watercress sauce (page 272) around each.

Kedgeree

Kedgeree is such a very British dish, yet it has its origins in India. It is imperative that kedgeree is always made with smoked fish. I deplore the recipes I have seen given by eminent chefs who use white fish for both kedgeree and fishcakes – both dishes are so bland when smoked fish is not used. Kedgeree can be made with smoked haddock, as in this recipe, or with hot-smoked salmon for a more special occasion – we always serve hot-smoked salmon and quails' egg kedgeree for brunch on New Year's Day, for instance. Smoked haddock kedgeree (or, for that matter, hot-smoked salmon kedgeree) can be dressed up with hollandaise sauce. Don't be put off by the teaspoon of curry powder you will see in the recipe: it makes all the difference to the taste. And kedgeree freezes beautifully – but without the hardboiled eggs; add those when you reheat it. Egg just turns to rubber when frozen.

Serves 6

675 g/1½ lb smoked haddock
600 ml/1 pint milk plus 600 ml/1 pint water (1.2 litres/2 pints total)
3 tbsps olive oil and 25 g/1 oz butter
2 medium-sized onions, skinned then finely and neatly diced
1 tsp medium-strength curry powder
375 g/12 oz long-grain rice – I use basmati
75 g/3 oz butter, cut in bits
4 hardboiled eggs, shelled and chopped
lots of black pepper
2 tbsps chopped parsley – an essential
ingredient for both taste and colour

Feel the fish and remove any bones you find – you can feel bones where it is impossible to see them. Cut the fish into small chunks about 2.5 cm/1 inch in size. Put the fish into a saucepan, add the milk and the water and heat gently until the liquid just reaches a gentle simmer. Take the pan off the heat and let the fish cool in the hot liquid.

Kedgeree

Heat the oil and butter together in a sauté pan (one which has a lid – you will need this in a minute!) and fry the diced onions for 3–4 minutes, stirring occasionally until the onions are quite soft and transparent-looking. Stir in the curry powder and the rice. Stir the rice around until each grain is coated with oil. Then pour in the liquid from the fish saucepan, but do not let any pieces of cooked fish into the sauté pan at this stage, because they will become overcooked and shredded as the rice cooks. Let the liquid bubble around the rice, don't stir again, cover the pan with a tea-towel then with the lid, and cook on a gentle heat for 5 minutes; then draw the pan off the heat and leave for 20–25 minutes. Don't be tempted to lift the lid. The rice will cook, absorbing the liquid as it does so. After this cooking time, fork the cooked fish and the bits of butter through the rice. Add the chopped hardboiled eggs if you are eating the kedgeree straight away, season well with black pepper and stir in the chopped parsley just before serving. This kedgeree will keep warm for a limited length of time, covered, in a warm oven.

To reheat from frozen, thaw and tip the kedgeree (frozen *without* the hardboiled eggs) into a well-buttered ovenproof dish – you could in fact freeze it in such a dish. Cover the surface with buttered baking parchment and then with a lid. Reheat the thawed kedgeree in a moderate oven, 180°C/350°F/gas mark 4 (bottom-right oven in a four-door Aga), for 25–30 minutes, forking the melting butter through from time to time and re-covering each time. Mix in the chopped hardboiled eggs and serve.

Scrambled eggs with Arbroath Smokies

This, made and served in smaller amounts, makes a perfect savoury. In this recipe, though, I am assuming it will be a lunch or supper dish. Arbroath Smokies are hot-smoked, therefore need no further cooking themselves; they just need the flesh flaked from their bones and skin, which are both then thrown away. The flakes of smoked fish are stirred through the scrambled eggs just before serving. If you like, you can spoon the mixture on top of buttered toast (granary, for my liking) or serve toast and butter separately. The eggs can be beaten up ready for scrambling a day in advance. The Arbroath Smokies can be flaked and skin and bones removed a day in advance, providing that the fish is kept in a closely covered bowl in the fridge overnight, to prevent it from drying out.

Serves 6

110 g/4 oz butter
12 large eggs
4 tbsps milk, or single cream if you prefer
a pinch of salt (no more – the fish will contribute saltiness)
a good grinding of black pepper
a dash of Tabasco
4 Arbroath Smokies, the flesh carefully removed from the skin and bones (pick out as many bones as you can)

Melt the butter in a large non-stick saucepan – which makes washing up so much easier. Meanwhile, beat the eggs very well, adding the milk, salt, pepper and Tabasco. Pour this into the melted butter in the pan and, over a gentle to moderate heat, cook, stirring continuously until the eggs are softly setting. Stir in the flaked Arbroath Smokies and dish up on to warmed plates. Eat immediately.

Smoked haddock, bacon and tomato omelette

This is a recipe for a sustaining breakfast, lunch or supper. It combines smoked haddock, which is first cooked and flaked from any bones and skin, then spooned over the surface of the just-cooked omelette before it is folded over, with grilled bacon and grilled or baked halved tomatoes.

You will notice that this recipe serves only 2, whereas most serve 6, but omelettes can be very anti-social if the poor cook is making them in relays. Half the people eating them will have finished before the others have had their omelettes cooked. But they are perfect as a dish for two.

Serves 2

450 g/1 lb Finnan haddock
milk to poach the fish
4 rashers best back bacon – dry-cured, smoked or unsmoked
2 tomatoes
a pinch of salt
a pinch of caster sugar
a good grinding of black pepper
25 g/1 oz butter, cut in half
4 large eggs, beaten well together with 2 tbsps cold water
**   and seasoned with salt and freshly ground pepper**
1 heaped tbsp chopped parsley and snipped chives, mixed

Put the haddock in a saucepan with just enough milk to cover it and poach for 1 minute. Remove from the heat and cool, then flake the fish, removing and discarding all the bones and skin. Set the flaked fish on one side.

Grill the bacon and, meanwhile, cut each tomato in half, then put them on a baking tray. Season each half with a pinch of salt, a pinch of caster sugar, a grinding of black pepper and a tiny piece of the butter. Grill under a half-hot grill until the tomatoes are quite soft. If you cook in an Aga, bake them in the moderate oven – bottom-right in a four-door Aga.

Heat half the remaining butter in an omelette pan over a fairly high heat, swirling the butter around. It will not be enough to quite cover the base – it isn't meant to. Mix the chopped parsley and snipped chives into the beaten eggs, and pour half this mixture into the omelette pan. Leave the base to set, then, with a knife, carefully lift up the edges of the omelette to let the egg mixture run underneath the set base. It, too, will set. When the surface of the omelette is just cooked but still soft, cover with half of the flaked, cooked smoked haddock and flip one half of the omelette over the other, to form a half-moon shape. Slip this on to a warmed plate and keep it warm while you repeat the process to make the second omelette. Serve, with the bacon rashers and grilled tomatoes at the side of each omelette.

Smoked haddock fishcakes

People of all ages love a good fishcake – I think it is the combination of the crispy exterior with the soft inside of each cake. And they are convenient!

Serves 6

675 g/1½ lb smoked haddock
675 g/1½ lb creamy, well-mashed potatoes (about 1.2kg/2½ lb in
   weight before cooking)
2 rounded tbsps finely chopped parsley
freshly ground black pepper
2 eggs, beaten in a shallow dish
50–75 g/2–3 oz fresh breadcrumbs
oil for frying (I use sunflower or olive)

Flake the cooked fish and remove any skin and bones. Mix together well the fish, the mashed potatoes and the parsley, and season with several grinds of black pepper. Form into balls of even size and flatten into cake shapes. Line a baking tray with siliconized grease-proof paper. Coat each cake in the beaten egg, drain it a little, and dip it into the breadcrumbs. Lay the breadcrumbed cakes on the lined baking tray. Put them in the refrigerator until you are ready to cook them. If you want to freeze them, do so at this stage. Give them a couple of hours to thaw.

When you are ready to cook the fishcakes, pour oil to a depth of about 1 cm/½ inch into a frying pan (less if the pan is non-stick) and heat it gently. Cook the fishcakes for 2–3 minutes on each side, until they are golden brown. Keep them warm on an ovenproof dish lined with two or three thicknesses of kitchen paper to absorb excess oil.

first courses or savouries, lunch or supper dishes

Crab tart with Parmesan pastry

Serves 6

For the pastry

110 g/4 oz butter, hard from the
fridge, cut into bits
1 tsp icing sugar
175 g/6 oz plain flour
½ tsp salt
a good grinding of black pepper
50 g /2 oz freshly grated
Parmesan cheese
1 tsp dried pink peppercorns

For the filling

2 large eggs
2 egg yolks
300 ml/½ pint double cream
2 tsps lemon juice
½ tsp Tabasco
½ tsp salt
a good grinding of black pepper
450 g /1 lb crabmeat, of the best
quality, and evenly mixed
brown and white crabmeat

Put the pastry ingredients into a food processor and whiz till it is the texture of fine crumbs. Press this mixture firmly around the sides and base of a flan dish or tin, measuring about 22 cm/9 inches in diameter, and put this into the fridge for at least 1 hour. Then bake in a moderate oven, 180°C/350°F/gas mark 4 (bottom-right oven in a four-door Aga), for 20–25 minutes. The pastry should just be shrinking away from the sides of the dish. Should the pastry slip down the sides, press it back up using the back of a metal spoon.

To make the filling, beat together the eggs and yolks, and beat in the cream, lemon juice, Tabasco and salt and pepper. Mix the crabmeat into this very thoroughly, and pour this mixture into the baked, cooled Parmesan pastry case. Bake in a moderate oven, 180°C/350°F/gas mark 4 (bottom-right oven in a four-door Aga), for 15–20 minutes, or until the centre of the filling is firm to touch – the centre is the last part to set during the cooking time.

Serve warm, or cold, with vinaigrette-dressed mixed salad leaves.

Main courses
and friends

or family

THIS CHAPTER INCLUDES RECIPES for an easy, family-and-friends style of eating, whether for lunch or supper. There are recipes such as Fish Pie, Leeks, Apples and Fish with Ginger, Fish Florentine (that useful and delicious combination of fish with spinach, seasoned with nutmeg and covered with cheese sauce) – these and so many more ideas for meals using fish as the main theme. We can, should and, in many cases, do eat several species of fish which we wouldn't have thought of eating twenty-five years ago – ling, for example, and megrim. If you see fish with strange names for sale in fishmongers or in supermarkets that have wet-fish counters, ask, and look at the fish – which will almost invariably be filleted or, if not, the fish merchant will fillet for you. So many of these are white-fleshed, fairly firm-fleshed, and very good. Fish is such convenient food and so very good for us. I can't imagine a week passing without at least four fish main courses and often, for us, there are seven!

Cod with fennel and bacon

My sister, Camilla Westwood, gave me this recipe. She invented it, and when I made it I loved it – the flavours of fennel, bacon and tomatoes all complement the fish so very well. I used this recipe in the Field, *when I wrote for them, and it produced an outraged letter from a reader who lived in Hampshire. She said that I should know better than to advocate the use of cod, that we should never buy cod. So I rang Andy Race, one of our three fish merchants, whose advice I respect highly. I thought I knew what I should respond to this lady, and I ran it past Andy, who endorsed my beliefs. They are these: cod is a by-catch of prawns, so it is inevitable that, where prawns are caught, so too will be cod. It seems so pointless, therefore, not to buy cod when you see it for sale – after all, it is dead, and therefore it might as well be eaten. But you can use any type of white fish in this recipe – hake, monkfish, whiting or ling, to give just four options.*

Postscript: organically farmed cod from the waters around Shetland appeared in shops in June 2006 and is proving to be a great success.

Serves 6

4 heads of fennel, ends trimmed off and the fennel
sliced thickly
4 large, or 6 smaller leeks, trimmed of ends and outer
leaves and sliced quite thickly diagonally
6 rashers of back bacon, fat trimmed off and the bacon
sliced into strips (use scissors)
5 tbsps olive oil
½ tsp salt (no more because of the bacon)
lots of black pepper
6 pieces of thick cod, or loin of cod, each weighing about 175 g/6 oz

In a non-stick roasting tin mix the prepared fennel, leeks and bacon strips thoroughly with the olive oil, and spread evenly within the roasting tin. Roast in a hot oven, 200°C/400°F/gas mark 6 (roasting oven in an Aga), for 20 minutes, then stir up the contents and re-spread everything to roast for a further 15–20 minutes. After this the fennel should be soft. Season with salt and pepper, and mix the

Cod with Fennel and Bacon

seasonings in thoroughly. Press each bit of cod down amongst the roast vegetables and roast in the oven for a further 10–15 minutes – it is impossible to be exact because the thickness of the cod varies, but test after 10 minutes, gently forking apart a piece of fish in its thickest part; if it parts easily into fat flakes it is cooked. Serve.

I love this with very well mashed potatoes, beaten with, if you like, lots of chopped parsley and snipped chives. There is no need for any more vegetables, but, if you like, a dressed mixed-leaf salad would be very good.

main courses for family and friends

Filleted cod with puy lentils, pickled lemons and tomatoes

You can use any firm-fleshed white fish for this instead of cod – hake, for example, or whiting, megrim, or ling. The tastes of the pickled lemons and tomatoes are so good together, and the lentils are delicious with the sharp, fruity flavours.

The only thing is that pickled lemons need to be made at least 3 weeks before using them – once opened, the jar must be kept in the fridge and will last for up to a year. Pickling lemons is simplicity itself. First, wash the lemons very well under running water to remove their preservative. Then, on a board, cut each lemon down in quarters but without cutting through the base of each. Push each lemon into a jar, adding 1 tablespoon of flaky salt (I use Maldon), trying to get as much of the salt as you can inside each lemon. Then pour boiling water into the jar up to the top and seal the jar. I find Kilner jars the best for this. Do not open the jars for 3–4 weeks.

This dish really has everything in it – starch in the lentil content, vegetables in the onions and tomatoes, but if you feel further vegetables are needed, I would eat spinach, wilted and seasoned with nutmeg.

Serves 6

4 tbsps olive oil

3 medium-sized onions, skinned and sliced thinly

1–2 fat cloves of garlic, skinned and finely chopped

3 tins of chopped tomatoes, each weighing 400 g/15 oz

1 tbsp quite finely chopped pickled lemon

lots of black pepper (no salt: the pickled lemon contributes enough saltiness)

6 pieces of filleted cod, each weighing about 175 g/6 oz

2 tbsps olive oil *For the lentils*

1 onion, skinned and finely diced

225 g/8 oz puy lentils

900 ml/1½ pints chicken or vegetable stock

Filleted cod with puy lentils, pickled lemons and tomatoes

Start by cooking the lentils. Heat the 2 tablespoons of olive oil in a saucepan and fry the diced onion in the oil for 2–3 minutes. Stir in the lentils, then add the stock. Let the stock reach simmering point and simmer gently, the pan uncovered, and stirring from time to time, for 20–25 minutes.

Meanwhile, in another saucepan or sauté pan, heat the 4 table-spoons of olive oil and fry the thinly sliced onions for several minutes, stirring occasionally so that they cook evenly. Cook until the onions are quite soft and beginning to turn colour at their edges. Then add the chopped garlic, and the contents of the tins of tomatoes. Let this mixture simmer gently, add the chopped pickled lemon and season with pepper. Simmer for 5 minutes, then push the pieces of fish down into the sauce, and bring the contents of the pan back to simmering point. Cook gently for 5 minutes – the fish will cook in the heat of the tomato mixture. Serve, with the lentils spooned beside or underneath.

You can get ahead by cooking the onions, tomatoes and pickled lemons a day ahead, reheating it to serve, and cooking the fish in the sauce at that point. You can even, if it is more convenient, cook the lentils and reheat them, but they look rather unappealing when cold, so don't let that put you off!

main courses for family and friends

Baked cod with onions and oranges

I love this combination of tastes. I also love this dish with mashed potatoes and buttery nutmeg-seasoned spinach, which goes very well with the onion and orange content of the recipe.

The fish and also the oranges can be prepared, and the onions can be fried till soft, a day ahead, so that the actual cooking of the whole dish only takes minutes.

Instead of cod, you could use any other firm-fleshed fish, such as hake, ling, salmon, megrim or whiting.

Serves 6

4 tbsps olive oil
4 medium-sized onions, skinned and sliced finely
1–2 cloves of garlic, skinned and chopped finely (optional)
6 oranges
2 tbsps chopped mint (applemint when in season)
6 pieces of filleted cod, each weighing about 175 g/6 oz
½ tsp salt
a good grinding of black pepper
1 tbsp strong soy sauce

Rub an ovenproof dish with butter or olive oil.

In a large sauté pan heat the olive oil and fry the thinly sliced onions and chopped garlic till they are very soft and transparent – stirring from time to time, to make sure they cook evenly. This will take about 5–7 minutes over a moderately high heat. Put some of the fried onions and garlic over the base of the dish.

Slice the skin from the oranges with a serrated knife and then cut each orange into 5 or 6 thin slices, reserving the juice. Put half the

Baked cod with onions and oranges

sliced oranges over the onion and garlic in the dish, and scatter the mint over the orange slices. Put the pieces of fish on this, and put the rest of the onions and garlic over the fish and the remainder of the oranges over the top. Mix the salt, pepper and soy sauce into the orange juice reserved from slicing the oranges, and pour this over the contents of the dish. Bake in a moderate heat, 180°C/350°/gas mark 4 (bottom-right oven in a four-door Aga), for 35–40 minutes. If the dish has been prepared in advance and kept in the fridge, do remember to take it into room temperature for half an hour before baking it.

Baked fillet of cod with bacon and broad beans in parsley sauce

*All these ingredients go together very well, both in flavour and in texture. But the broad beans **must** be as young as possible and not those large card-board-textured broad beans that give this vegetable a bad name. I prefer to grill streaky bacon, rather than back bacon. The only things needed to round off this delicious repast are steamed new potatoes with mint.*

Serves 6

6 pieces of filleted cod, each weighing about 175 g/6 oz
50 g/2 oz butter
2 fairly level tbsps flour
750 ml/1¼ pints milk
½ tsp salt
a good grinding of black pepper
a grating of nutmeg
450 g/1 lb podded broad beans
3 tbsps chopped parsley, either flat-leaved or curly
18 rashers of best-quality, thinly sliced streaky bacon, smoked or unsmoked, grilled as crisp as you like

Feel the pieces of cod and remove any bones you encounter. Line a baking tray with a sheet of baking parchment, put the prepared pieces of cod on this, cover with another sheet of baking parchment and bake in a moderate oven, 180°C/350°F/gas mark 4 (bottom-right oven in a four-door Aga), for 15–20 minutes – how long depends on the thickness of the fish.

Melt the butter in a saucepan and stir in the flour. Let this cook for a minute before gradually adding the milk, stirring all the time until

Baked fillet of cod with bacon and
broad beans in parsley sauce

the sauce boils. Season with salt, pepper and nutmeg, then draw the pan off the heat. Meanwhile, steam the broad beans until tender – if the beans are as small as they should be, this takes the same length of time as it will take you to make the white sauce. Tip the steamed beans into the seasoned sauce, and stir in the chopped parsley – don't be tempted to add less, as this sauce is meant to be full of parsley.

Serve the steam-baked fish with the grilled bacon on top, and with the broad beans in parsley sauce either spooned beside or handed separately.

Roast cod with roast aubergines and shallots, with tomato and garlic mayonnaise

Serves 6

5 aubergines, ends cut off and the aubergines cut into chunks
about 5 cm/2 inches in size
6 banana or torpedo shallots, with violet-tinted flesh,
skinned and quartered
6 tbsps olive oil
1 tsp salt
a good grinding of black pepper
½ tsp dried chilli flakes
6 pieces of filleted cod, each weighing about 175 g/6 oz
1 batch tomato and garlic mayonnaise (page 252)

Put the chunks of aubergine and quartered shallots on to a roasting tin (line it first, if you like, with a sheet of baking parchment – this makes washing up quicker) and mix in the olive oil, salt, pepper and chilli. This is only really thoroughly done by hand. Spread them evenly on the roasting tin and roast in a hot oven, 200°C/400°F/gas mark 6 (roasting oven in an Aga), for 20 minutes. Then shuffle the vegetables around on the roasting tin and continue to roast for a further 20 minutes – or more, if the chunks of aubergine aren't quite soft and beginning to turn golden at the edges. You can do this several hours in advance if you like. Then reheat till very hot, and push the pieces of fish down into the roast aubergines and shallots,

Roast cod with roast aubergines and shallots, with tomato and garlic mayonnaise

cover the top with a sheet of baking parchment and cook, at the same temperature, for 5 minutes. Check, by sticking a knife into the thickest part of a piece of fish, to see that it falls into flakes and isn't undercooked. The time varies according to the thickness of the fish. Continue to cook if the fish isn't ready.

Serve, with the Tomato and Garlic Mayonnaise handed separately. I love steamed new potatoes with mint with this – the mint is so good with the fish as well as with the potatoes. A mixed-leaf salad is the only other accompaniment necessary.

Baked cod with spiced lentils and coriander pesto

This is a lovely combination of tastes and a most convenient dish to make, because everything bar actually baking the fish can be done ahead – and the fish can be made ready hours in advance just to pop into the oven. So all that is needed before eating is to heat up the lentils as the fish cooks, then assemble it all to serve.

Serves 6

6 pieces of filleted cod, weighing about 175 g/6 oz each
75 g/3 oz butter, cut into 6 bits
juice and grated rind of 1 lime, washed well to remove preservative and dried before grating

For the pesto

2 cloves of garlic, skinned and chopped
50 g/2 oz pine nuts, dry-fried to toast them, and cooled
2 packets of fresh coriander
150 ml/¼ pint olive oil
juice of 1 lime
½ tsp salt
a good grinding of black pepper

2 tbsps olive oil
2 onions, skinned and finely diced
1 chilli, slit open, seeded and finely sliced
175 g/6 oz green puy lentils
600 ml/1 pint vegetable stock
½ tsp salt
a good grinding of black pepper

For the green lentils

Baked cod with spiced lentils and coriander pesto

Make the pesto first, because it will keep in the fridge for 2–3 days. Put the garlic and pine nuts into a food processor and whiz, adding the coriander as it whizzes. In a thin, steady trickle add the olive oil as it whizzes, and the lime juice, salt and pepper. Scoop and scrape this into a bowl or jar, cover and put in the fridge till required.

Next, prepare the lentils. Heat the oil in a saucepan and add the finely diced onions and the chilli. Cook over a moderate heat until the onions and chilli are very soft and beginning to turn golden, then stir in the lentils. Pour in the stock, season with salt and pepper, and bring the liquid to simmering point. Cover the pan and cook gently until the lentils are quite soft and the liquid has been absorbed to a great extent.

For the fish, cover a baking tray with baking parchment. Put the pieces of fish on this, removing any bones you feel as you do so. Put a bit of butter on each, sprinkle the lime juice and rind over the fish, cover with another piece of baking parchment and bake in a moderate oven, 180°C/350°F/gas mark 4 (bottom-right oven in a four-door Aga), until cooked – anything from 10 to 20 minutes. The variation in time depends so much on the thickness of the cod – smaller but thicker bits need longer cooking time than larger, flatter pieces of fish. Test for doneness by gently forking apart the thickest part of a piece of fish with two forks.

To serve, spoon some lentils on to each of six warmed plates. Put a piece of fish on top and a good teaspoonful of the coriander pesto on the fish. Serve.

main courses for family and friends

Crab cakes

These can be a first course, in smaller size, but I think that they are so filling, so delicious that they make a much better main course. They are convenient because they can be made a day in advance, but they must be kept on a covered tray in the fridge until you are ready to fry them. They can be accompanied by a variety of the sauces from the Sauces, Salsas and Accompaniments chapter, either hot or cold, but my choice is a mayonnaise, and the Tomato and Garlic Mayonnaise (page 252) above all else. New potatoes and a good salad would make this the perfect main course.

I usually love half and half white and brown crabmeats in almost every crab recipe. But for crab cakes we need a predominance of white, because the brown in any more quantity makes the mixture too soft to form into cakes. If you are short of crab you can, if you like, add more brown breadcrumbs to the crabmeat in the bowl instead of some of the crab.

Serves 6

900 g/2 lb crabmeat, of which ¾ should be white and ¼ brown
2 slices of brown bread, whizzed in a food processor to
give 50 g/2 oz crumbs
1 tsp Tabasco
2 tbsps Worcester sauce
½ tsp salt, preferably Maldon
a good grinding of black pepper

225 g/8 oz brown breadcrumbs *For the coating*
1 tbsp chopped parsley, mixed through the crumbs

Line a large plastic tray with baking parchment.

Put the crabmeats into a large bowl and mix them together well, keeping an eye out for any small bits of shell which may have escaped into the crabmeat. Mix in the crumbs from the two slices of brown bread, the Tabasco, Worcester sauce, salt and pepper, mixing all together very well. If you have those close-fitting vinyl gloves, that will make the cake-making much less messy and easier by far. You

Crab cakes

want to make 12 cakes, so divide the mixture into four in the bowl, knowing that you want to get 3 cakes from each amount; this helps get the crab cakes more or less the same size. Form the cakes, then press each gently on either side into the breadcrumbs and parsley.

Put the coated crab cakes on to the baking parchment-lined plastic tray and, when they are all made up, cover with a second sheet of parchment, cover that with clingfilm and put the tray into the fridge for several hours, or overnight.

Heat olive oil to just cover the base of a non-stick sauté pan and, when the oil is hot, fry the crab cakes in batches. Once you put the cakes into the hot oil, leave them. Don't be tempted to move them around in the sauté pan – this prevents them from frying completely on their base, and causes them to break up. Leave them alone for 1 minute before carefully turning them over to cook on their other side for a further minute. As they cook, remove them to a warm oven-proof dish, lined with a couple of thicknesses of kitchen paper. Serve them warm.

Smoked and fresh haddock quenelles with chive cream sauce

I make no apology for repeating two quenelle recipes in this book – the haddock recipe below, and the salmon recipe on pages 145–6; these both appeared in my book Entertaining Solo. *The reason I repeat them is that they belong in a book on fish, because there must be very many of you who, like me, thought that making quenelles was for chefs, that they were fraught with potential difficulty, when, of course, they are anything but. If I can make them, anyone can. And I couldn't ever have thought of making them had I not been lucky enough to be staying with my friends the Thewes, where Henrietta (a brilliant cook, as, too, are both her sisters) was making quenelles which we then ate for dinner. She showed me how easy they are – and they really are! Henrietta knocked up her quenelles with such apparent ease that I came home filled with inspiration and I've been making them ever since. All thanks to her!*

You can make up the quenelle mixture a day in advance, if that is more convenient for you. They take literally 5 minutes to poach – a bit longer if you do a large panful of them, but only by a couple of minutes. They keep warm in their sauce, most obligingly, for 30–45 minutes.

Serves 6

450 g/1 lb smoked haddock, filleted
225 g/8 oz fresh haddock, filleted
1 large egg
2 egg whites
300 ml/½ pint double cream
15 g/½ oz or so parsley
a good grinding of black pepper
a grating of nutmeg
stock, made from water and Marigold vegetable
stock powder (see method for quantity required)

300 ml/½ pint double cream *For the sauce*
1 tbsp lemon juice
2 tbsps snipped chives

Smoked and fresh haddock
quenelles with chive cream sauce

Make the quenelles mixture by putting both fish into a food processor and whizzing, adding the egg and the egg whites, the cream, the parsley and the pepper and nutmeg. Whiz till smooth and green-flecked with the parsley. Scrape this mixture into a bowl, cover, and put the bowl into the fridge for 3–4 hours, or overnight.

In a saucepan (or a sauté pan) heat stock to a depth of 6–7.5 cm/2½–3 inches. When it is fast boiling, with two tablespoons form neat and even egg shapes of the fish mixture, and slip them into the boiling stock. Poach the quenelles for 5 minutes, turning them over during their cooking time. As they poach, butter or rub with olive oil an ovenproof dish, and put the poached quenelles into this as they are cooked.

Make the simple cream sauce by putting the cream, lemon juice and snipped chives into a saucepan, bring to simmering point, and, stirring, boil for 2 minutes. Pour this over the finished quenelles – it just coats their surface. Cover the dish and keep it warm until you are ready to serve.

Baked haddock with parsley, garlic and lemon pesto

A friend who used to live in Granada gave this recipe to me. Local friends in Spain taught her this. It is so good, and is a regular dish for us on a Tuesday, when Sean, our Buckie-based fish merchant calls with his fish van. You can prepare it several hours ahead, but closely cover the dish with clingfilm before putting it into the fridge, because the garlic is fairly pronounced! This isn't an elegant dish, but it tastes very good. Boiled potatoes, either new or old, or mashed potatoes are good with this dish. What with the parsley content of the pesto and the tomatoes on top, there isn't much need for another vegetable, except a mixed-leaf salad.

Instead of haddock, you could use any other white fish you like.

Serves 6

1.2 kg/2 lb filleted haddock
110 g/4 oz parsley, flat-leaved or curly
2 fat cloves of garlic, skinned and chopped
½ tsp dried chilli flakes (optional)
finely grated rind of 1 lemon, washed well to remove
preservative and dried before grating
300 ml/½ pint olive oil
1 tbsp lemon juice
½ tsp salt
a good grinding of black pepper
450 g/1 lb cherry tomatoes, washed and cut in half

Baked haddock with parsley, garlic and lemon pesto

Put the fish fillets on a board and slit either side of the row of tiny bones you will encounter down the middle of each. Feel also at the outer top edges, as usually there is a tiny amount of bones there too. Cut them out. Put the trimmed fish into an ovenproof dish.

Put the parsley into a food processor, with the chopped garlic, chilli flakes and lemon rind and whiz, slowly adding the olive oil. Whiz in the lemon juice, salt and pepper. Scrape out the contents of the processor and spread it over the entire surface of the fish. Dot the halved cherry tomatoes over. Bake in a moderate heat, 180°C/350°F/ gas mark 4 (bottom-right oven in a four-door Aga), for 35–40 minutes. It will keep warm without spoiling for about half an hour.

Smoked haddock and leek au gratin

The idea for this was given to me by the wonderful chef Rosemary Shrager.
You can add bits of bacon to the sliced leeks as they fry to soften, if you like.
The taste of bacon with fish of all types, both smoked and unsmoked, is
delicious. This is a convenient supper or lunch dish. It can be prepared a day
in advance and kept, with the dish covered, in the fridge. Allow 30 minutes
at room temperature before reheating it. I like boiled basmati rice with this,
and, possibly, a mixed-leaf salad dressed with a vinaigrette containing Dijon
mustard – good with the cheese content of this dish.

Serves 6

1.2kg/2½ lb smoked haddock (not the hideous dyed kind,
but the very best you can buy)
1.2 litres/2 pints milk
4 tbsps olive oil
6 medium-sized leeks, trimmed of ends and outer
leaves and sliced thinly
2 fairly level tbsps flour
1 tsp Dijon mustard
a good grinding of black pepper (no salt, the smoked haddock will
contribute enough saltiness)
a grating of nutmeg
175 g/6 oz grated best Cheddar, Lancashire or Gruyère
(whichever you prefer; we use Mull Cheddar)
50 g/2 oz breadcrumbs, brown or white
2 tbsps chopped parsley (optional, but very good
if you can include it)

Feel the fish on a board and remove any bones you find. Cut the fish
into bite-sized pieces, about 2.5 cm/1 inch in size. Put the pieces of fish
into a saucepan with the milk and, over a moderate heat, cook until the
milk comes to a simmering point. Take the pan off the heat and let
the fish cool in the milk, which also infuses the milk with the flavour of
the fish. Then, when cold, strain off the milk to make into the sauce.

Smoked haddock and leek au gratin

Heat the olive oil in a saucepan – non-stick if possible, to make washing up afterwards easier – and fry the thinly sliced leeks over a moderate heat. Stir the leeks from time to time, to make sure they cook evenly, and fry them for several minutes until they are quite soft – they will decrease in volume as they soften. Then stir in the flour, and let the flour and leeks cook for a minute. Stirring continuously, gradually add the milk reserved from cooking the fish. When all the milk is added, let the sauce boil, then draw the pan off the heat and stir in the Dijon mustard, pepper and nutmeg, and half the amount of grated cheese. Mix in the pieces of cooked smoked haddock, and put the contents of the pan into an ovenproof dish.

In a bowl, mix together the rest of the grated cheese with the breadcrumbs and chopped parsley, mixing thoroughly. When the fish and leeks have cooled in their sauce, scatter the cheese mixture evenly over the surface.

To reheat, cook in a moderate heat, 180°C/350°F/gas mark 4 (bottom-right oven in a four-door Aga), for 35–40 minutes, or until the cheese on the top has melted and formed a crust with the bread-crumbs, and the underneath is bubbling around the sides of the dish. Do remember, it is most important that the dish is not put into the oven straight from the fridge; it must be at room temperature for 30 minutes or so before reheating.

Smoked haddock and spinach cheese pie

This is one of those convenient recipes with everything you need in one great big dish. I put this together for supper one night – it is a sort of upside-down fish pie-cum-Florentine, but it really is very good. I have never frozen it, but you can make it a day in advance.

Serves 6

900 g/2 lb smoked haddock
1.2 litres/2 pints milk
1.35 kg/ 3 lb potatoes, weighed before peeling
1.35 kg/3 lb young spinach (not as much as it sounds:
it wilts down to very little)
2 tbsps olive oil
75 g/3 oz butter
2 just rounded tbsps flour
1 tsp Dijon mustard
225 g/8 oz grated good Cheddar cheese
salt
black pepper
nutmeg

Butter a large ovenproof dish thoroughly.

Feel the fish with your fingers and remove any bones you find; I cut either side of the line of bones. Cut the fish into pieces about 2.5 cm/1 inch in size. Put the pieces of fish into a saucepan with the milk. Over a moderate heat, bring the milk to simmering point, then take the pan off the heat and let the fish cool in the milk – it will infuse the milk with its flavour.

Peel the potatoes and boil them until tender. Drain them and steam them dry, then mash them well and season with salt, pepper and nutmeg. (Add butter if you like, but I don't think it is necessary.) Beat the mashed potatoes well with a wooden spoon to get a fluffy texture.

Smoked haddock and spinach cheese pie

Pack the spinach into a large pan, over a fairly high heat. Pour in a very small amount – about 300 ml/½ pint – of boiling water and clamp a lid on the pan. Within 2 minutes the spinach will have collapsed. Take the pan off the heat but leave the lid on, and let the contents of the pan cool. Then drain into a colander or large sieve, pressing the spinach down to squeeze out not only the cooking liquid but as much excess water as possible from the spinach itself. Put the well-drained spinach back into the pan and chop it (if the pan is not non-stick; if it is, chop the spinach in a bowl) and add the olive oil, salt, pepper and nutmeg.

Make the cheese sauce by melting the butter in a large saucepan. Stir in the flour and let this cook for a couple of minutes before gradually adding the reserved fish milk, stirring all the time until the sauce boils. Take the pan off the heat, season with Dijon mustard, pepper and nutmeg. Stir in half the grated cheese, stirring until it all melts.

Assemble the contents of the dish by putting the beaten mashed potatoes in the base of the buttered ovenproof dish. Put the seasoned chopped spinach over the potatoes, and put the pieces of fish over the spinach. Cover the fish with the cheese sauce and cover the surface with the rest of the grated cheese. At this stage you can cover the dish with clingfilm and put it in the fridge until the next day. Before reheating, remember to take the dish from the fridge into room temperature for half an hour, before removing the clingfilm. Bake the dish in a moderate heat, 180°C/350°F/gas mark 4 (bottom-right oven in a four-door Aga), for 40–45 minutes. The surface cheese should be molten golden brown and the sauce should be bubbling well.

main courses for family and friends

Smoked haddock, shallot, spinach and saffron stew

I have done this recipe so many times at cooking demonstrations up and down the country. We are all told frequently that we should reduce the fat in our diets, and I am all for that, but once in a while we can splurge – and this recipe is so simple, so utterly delicious and I have received so many compliments about it that it is well worth a splurge. All that's needed to go with it are boiled potatoes; otherwise everything for a whole main course is in the saucepan!

It goes without saying that the smoked haddock you use should be undyed!

Serves 6

900 g–1.2 kg/2–2½ lb filleted smoked haddock
8–10 shallots (depending on their size), finely chopped
3 tbsps extra-virgin olive oil
600 ml/1 pint double cream
2 good pinches of saffron strands (about ½ tsp)
plenty of black pepper (no salt: the fish should be sufficiently salty)
110 g/4 oz baby spinach leaves

Put the smoked haddock on a board and feel it carefully with your fingertips; cut out any bones that you detect. Cut the fish into chunks about 4 cm/1½ inches in size.

Skin and chop the shallots very finely. Heat the olive oil in a large sauté pan and sauté the finely chopped shallots until they are quite soft. Then add the pieces of fish, the cream and saffron, and bring it to a gentle simmer. The fish will take about 3 minutes to cook, depending to a certain extent on the width of your sauté pan. Season with pepper, add the spinach – it will be a high mound, but cover the

Smoked haddock, shallot, spinach and saffron stew

pan with a lid and the spinach will wilt very quickly. When it has wilted right down, carefully – so as not to break up the pieces of fish more than you can help – combine it evenly with the rest of the contents of the sauté pan. Ladle into warmed bowls to serve.

You can prepare your fish hours in advance – or the previous day. Keep it in a covered bowl in the fridge. Similarly, you can chop and sauté the shallots well in advance. So all you need to do before eating is to assemble the ingredients and cook them.

main courses for family and friends

Smoked haddock and grilled goat's cheese on herb risotto

This is our idea of a perfect supper main course. It is fairly filling, but all the tastes combine very well indeed. All that's needed by way of an accompaniment is a mixed-leaf salad, dressed with Dijon mustardy vinaigrette.

For me, the herbs in this dish are usually parsley and snipped chives, sometimes also dill and occasionally chervil; add whatever you like (I, for instance, loathe tarragon so I never add it, but if you like it, do by all means include it).

Serves 6

6 pieces of filleted, undyed smoked haddock, each weighing about 175 g/6 oz
6 slices of goat's cheese, each weighing about 50 g/2 oz

For the risotto

4 tbsps olive oil
2 medium-sized onions, skinned and diced finely
1–2 cloves of garlic, skinned and chopped finely
375 g/12 oz risotto rice (arborio or carnaroli)
150 ml/¼ pint dry white wine
1.5 litres/2½ pints chicken or vegetable stock
½ tsp salt
a good grinding of black pepper
110 g/4 oz herbs, chopped quite finely

Put the fillets of fish on a board and feel them carefully for bones, removing any that you discover.

Put a sheet of baking parchment on a baking tray. Put the pieces of smoked haddock on this and cover with a second sheet of baking parchment, ready to bake in a moderate oven, 180°C/350°F/gas mark 4 (bottom-right oven in a four-door Aga), for 15–20 minutes, depending on the thickness of the fish. You will need to bake the fish towards the end of the risotto-making.

Smoked haddock and grilled goat's cheese on herb risotto

Heat the olive oil in a large sauté pan and fry the diced onions for several minutes, stirring to make sure they cook evenly, until the onions are quite soft and transparent-looking. Then add the garlic and cook for a minute before adding the rice. Stir the rice around, over heat, for 2–3 minutes – the aim is to coat each grain of rice with olive oil. Then stir in the white wine. Let this bubble till it has evaporated, then slowly add the stock, a small amount at a time, stirring, and letting it bubble gently and reduce right down before adding some more. Season with salt and pepper. Don't try to hurry this – making risotto is very soothing, I find. When all the stock has been added, the fish should be cooked.

Put a piece of foil over the grill pan of your cooker and lightly brush it with oil. Put the slices of goat's cheese on this and get ready to cook them briefly by putting them under a pre-heated red-hot grill for barely 1 minute, watching them like a hawk. Don't think to turn over the slices of goat's cheese – they need only grill till the surface of one side speckles golden brown and the cheese starts to melt. Goat's cheese melts quicker than does any other type of cheese: be warned!

Stir the chopped herbs through the risotto, and assemble by spooning some risotto on to each of six warmed plates. Put a piece of baked smoked haddock on top of the risotto, and put a slice of grilled goat's cheese on top of the fish. Eat immediately!

Smoked haddock Welsh rarebit

This delectable dish was inspired by Gary Rhodes. My version is different from his, and I can never make up my mind which I like best. I love the anchovies in mine, and you will see that mine has no breadcrumbs, but I definitely give him credit for the idea in the first place. He is one of the few top chefs whose food is delicious to watch being prepared on TV as well as being simple food that can be tackled by any domestic cook.

This recipe is best complemented by a tomato salad (dressed with a Dijon mustard vinaigrette) and spinach, wilted in olive oil and seasoned with salt, pepper and nutmeg. And serve with warm bread – granary bread is my idea of the perfect bread to go with this – or with most things, for that matter!

Serves 6

450 g/1 lb really good hard cheese (I use Mull Cheddar, grated; Lancashire is just as good)
300 ml/½ pint dry cider
4 anchovy fillets, drained and chopped quite small
2 large egg yolks
a good grinding of black pepper
a grating of nutmeg
a dash of Tabasco
2 tbsps chopped parsley and snipped chives, mixed
6 pieces of smoked haddock, each weighing about 175 g/ 6 oz

Put the grated cheese and the cider into a saucepan over a moderate heat. Stir until the cheese has melted in the heating cider. Stir in the chopped anchovy fillets. Beat the egg yolks together, mix into them a small amount of the hot cheese mixture, then scrape the yolks back into the saucepan and stir over a moderate heat for a couple of minutes. Take the pan off the heat. Stir in the pepper, nutmeg and Tabasco, and the chopped parsley and snipped chives.

Smoked haddock Welsh rarebit

Feel the fish on a board, and cut out and throw away any bones you encounter. Rub an ovenproof dish with olive oil, and put the pieces of fish into the dish. Spoon the cheese mixture over the fish, and put the dish under a fairly hot grill – don't have the grill on its highest heat, but about two-thirds hot. Grill until the surface of the cheese is turning into golden-brown speckles and is bubbling gently. This should take about 10 minutes. As the cheese mixture cooks under the heat of the grill, the fish cooks under the sauce.

The cheese mixture can be prepared a day in advance, but reheat it before spooning it over the fish, because otherwise it will be too stiff to do this with ease.

Pasta au gratin with smoked haddock, bacon and leeks

If you prefer, just leave the bacon out of this recipe, but it does go very well with the smoked haddock and leeks. This is such a convenient dish: everything in one, fish, vegetables and pasta, and all able to be made a day in advance – just my sort of main course! Choose whichever type of cheese you like for the gratin covering – a good Cheddar, or Lancashire, or Parmesan, which is what I suggest in the ingredients. A mixed-leaf salad, dressed with a mustardy vinaigrette, is the ideal accompaniment for this delicious pasta gratin.

Serves 6

900 g/2 lb best-quality smoked haddock (not the
bright-yellow dyed stuff)
1.2 litres/2 pints milk
4 rashers back bacon, dry-cured if possible
50 g/2 oz butter and 2 tbsps olive oil
6 medium-sized leeks, trimmed of outer leaves and
ends, and sliced thinly
2 tbsps flour
1 tsp Dijon mustard
a good grinding of black pepper
a grating of nutmeg
375 g/12 oz short pasta (e.g. bow shapes, shell
shapes or spirals)
2 tbsps olive oil
110 g/4 oz grated Parmesan

Feel the fish all over and remove all bones. Cut the fish into pieces about 2.5 cm/1 inch in size, and put them into a saucepan. Add the milk and, over a moderate heat, cook until the milk just begins to simmer. Take the pan off the heat and leave the fish to cool completely in the milk. Then strain the milk into a jug to make the sauce.

Pasta au gratin with smoked haddock, bacon and leeks

Trim the rim of fat from the bacon rashers and slice the rashers thinly. In a large saucepan (preferably one with a non-stick surface) melt the butter and heat it and the olive oil together. Add the sliced leeks and bacon. Over a fairly high heat, stir the leeks and bacon for several minutes, until the leeks are quite soft – this will take about 5 minutes. Then stir in the flour and let it cook for a minute before gradually adding the reserved milk, stirring all the time until all the milk is added and the sauce boils. Draw the pan off the heat and season with mustard, pepper and nutmeg – no need for salt; both the fish and the bacon contribute enough salt to the taste. Add the cooked fish to the leek mixture.

Meanwhile, boil water in a saucepan and add the pasta to the boiling water. Cook for 6 minutes from when the water returns to the boil, then drain the cooked pasta (which will have a slight bite to it – it's meant to) and mix a couple of tablespoons of olive oil through the drained pasta. Then tip this into the sauce, or the other way round, depending on which pan is bigger! Mix all together thoroughly and pour into an ovenproof dish. Scatter the grated cheese over the surface and either pop the dish under a hot grill until the cheese melts to form a golden crust, or cool the dish and its contents. Reheat in a moderate oven, 180°C/350°F/gas mark 4 (bottom-right oven in a four-door Aga), for 35–40 minutes, or until the cheese has melted and the sauce is bubbling around the edges. Beware putting the dish from the fridge into the oven – it will need much longer to reheat, which will not improve it. Take the dish from the fridge to room temperature half an hour before reheating.

main courses for family and friends

Herring in oatmeal with orange and shallot sauce

You can equally well use mackerel instead of herring for this. I always use pinhead oatmeal to coat fish, to make into a crust for racks of lamb, or to coat chicken breasts. I love the crunch of the fried pinhead oatmeal, but it must have some salt added to it before it is used to coat anything, even fish. The salt brings out the taste of the oatmeal – it is essential. The sharp orange sauce is the perfect accompaniment to either herring or mackerel. Herring have such a short season – about the end of June to early August – and we should make the most of them during this time.

This is fairly filling, whether herring or mackerel is the subject, and I personally never want potatoes to eat with it, but Godfrey does! Plain boiled potatoes, or steamed new ones in season, then, and peas, preferably fresh and podded by you in season, otherwise frozen. I love them!

Even though the herring are filleted, they will still have lots of small bones, but you can pick them out as you eat them.

Serves 6

6 herring, gutted and filleted
2 eggs, beaten on a plate
225 g/8 oz pinhead oatmeal, mixed well with ½ tsp salt
olive oil

3 large, or 6 smaller shallots, each skinned and diced very finely   *For the sauce*
300 ml/½ pint chicken or vegetable stock
150 ml/¼ pint lemon juice
1 tbsp granulated sugar
2 oranges, washed very well and dried
50 g/2 oz soft butter
2 fairly level tsps flour
½ tsp salt
lots of black pepper
1 tbsp chopped parsley

Herring in oatmeal with orange and shallot sauce

For the sauce, put the diced shallots into a saucepan with the stock. Simmer this gently for 5 minutes.

In another saucepan put the lemon juice and granulated sugar. Over a gentle moderate heat stir until the sugar has dissolved completely, then boil till the amount has reduced by half – it will almost caramelize. Stir this into the simmering stock and shallots.

Meanwhile, grate the orange rinds and then with a sharp serrated knife cut the pith left on the oranges after you have grated them. Throw away the pith. Chop the flesh, removing any pips you find, and put the chopped oranges and their rinds in a bowl.

Work the butter and flour together, add this mixture to the simmering stock and stir until it boils, adding the salt and black pepper. Then add the chopped oranges and rinds, and any juice collected from the oranges. Stir till the sauce boils again, take the pan off the heat and keep warm whilst you cook the herring.

Dip each herring in beaten egg then in the pinhead oatmeal. As you do this, lay them on a plastic tray.

To cook, heat the oil in a sauté pan, a tablespoon or two if it is a non-stick pan but a bit more if it isn't non-stick. Fry as many herring as you can fit into the pan at a time – this will probably be two. Turn them over after 1–2 minutes and cook on their other side for the same time. The coating should be golden brown and crisp. Lift them on to a warmed dish when they are cooked, then stir the chopped parsley into the sauce and serve with the herring.

Smoked mackerel and rice salad with curry and lime vinaigrette

I like to serve this salad on a large ashet or serving platter.

Serves 6

450 g/1 lb basmati rice
6 peppered mackerel fillets
6 eggs, *or* 12 quails' eggs, hardboiled, shelled and cut in half

For the dressing

5 tbsps extra-virgin olive oil
½ tsp salt
some freshly ground black pepper (not too much if using peppered smoked fish
2 tsps runny honey
1 rounded tsp medium-strength curry powder
juice and finely grated rind of 2 limes, washed well to remove preservative and dried before grating
2 tbsps mixed chopped parsley and snipped chives

Boil the rice in a large pan of salted water for about 7–8 minutes till just tender. Run cold water through the rice and drain thoroughly.

Flake the fish from its skin and remove any bones.

In a large bowl carefully mix together the flaked fish and drained cooked rice. In another bowl mix together the ingredients for the dressing. (When spooning the honey, dip the spoon in very hot water for a few seconds before putting it into the honey, which will then slip easily off the spoon.) Mix this dressing thoroughly through the fish and rice, and then heap on to the serving plate. Arrange the egg halves around, slightly pressed into the rice and fish.

Stir-fried Asian monkfish

This can be cooked in literally 5 minutes. Its preparation has to take place several hours ahead of cooking, but that can be done as much as a day in advance and the fish and its marinade kept in a covered bowl in the fridge overnight. But do remember to take everything into room temperature for half an hour before cooking. I like boiled basmati rice with this, and either a mixed-leaf salad or green beans.

Serves 6

150 ml/¼ pint medium sherry
150 ml/¼ pint strong soy sauce
3 tbsps sesame oil
1 fat clove of garlic, skinned and chopped finely
½ tsp caster sugar
½ tsp ground ginger
1.2 kg/2½ lb monkfish, trimmed of all membrane
   and cut into chunks about 2.5 cm/1 inch in size
4 tbsps olive oil

In a large bowl mix together the sherry, soy sauce, sesame oil, garlic, sugar and ginger. Then add the chunks of monkfish and mix well. Cover the bowl with clingfilm and keep in the fridge for 4 hours or overnight.

Strain the marinade into a measure jug and pat the monkfish chunks dry with kitchen paper.

Heat the olive oil in a large sauté pan and stir-fry the pieces of fish – they will spit a bit because it's impossible to dry them completely. Stir them around over the heat for a couple of minutes, then pour in the marinade and let this bubble for a further couple of minutes. Serve, spooned over boiled rice.

Barbecued or chargrilled monkfish with chilli roast aubergines

Monkfish is such a robust white fish; it can stand strong tastes and challenging cooking, as in barbecuing. If you are lucky enough to have an in-built chargrill in your kitchen, then you can cook this year round. On the other hand, have you seen the small Cobb's barbecue-cum-hot-smokers? They were designed for use in the galleys of boats, and I use mine in the kitchen and love it.

This is very good if accompanied by the Roast Red Pepper Sauce (page 258), as well as or instead of the Black Olive Relish (page 259).

Serves 6

1.2 kg/2½ lb monkfish fillets, trimmed of all membrane
3 fat cloves of garlic, skinned and finely sliced (optional)
½ tsp salt
a good grinding of black pepper
300 ml/½ pint olive oil

4 aubergines   *For the aubergines*
about 6 tbsps olive oil
½ tsp chilli flakes
1 level tsp salt, preferably Maldon

Start by preparing the monkfish for marinating: stick a knife down each fillet of monkfish in several places. Stuff a thin piece of garlic in these slits, and put the fish into a wide dish. Mix the salt and pepper into the olive oil, and pour this over the garlic-studded monkfish in the dish. Cover with clingfilm, and leave for several hours, or overnight, in the fridge.

Wipe each aubergine and cut off the green ends. Then cut the aubergines into chunks about 2.5 cm/1 inch in size and mix the pieces well with the olive oil, chilli flakes and salt.

Barbecued or chargrilled monkfish, with chilli roast aubergines

To roast the aubergine chunks, put the olive oil and salted pieces of aubergine on to a baking tray or roasting tin lined with a sheet of baking parchment if you wish – it does make washing up a breeze – and roast them in a hot oven, 200°C/400°F/gas mark 6 (roasting oven in an Aga), for 20 minutes. Then shuffle the pieces of aubergine around and continue to roast for a further 5–10 minutes, or until the pieces are collapsed and looking roasted. Take them out of the oven and keep them warm on a heated dish while the monkfish cooks.

Light a barbecue in very good time to allow the coals to burn through red and down to a white heat. Lift the pieces of fish from their olive-oil marinade and pat them with a wedge of kitchen paper to remove much of the surface oil, then put them on to the grill. Turn them after 25–30 seconds – the fish will firm up and turn opaque. Allow about 1 minute's cooking time in total, unless the monkfish fillets are very thick, in which case allow longer.

Spaghetti with mussels, tomatoes and capers

This is a variation on pasta alle vongole. *We have a mussel farm a couple of miles from Kinloch and the mussels are wonderful, large, plump and orange. For this recipe, the tomato and mussel sauce takes the same amount of time to cook as the pasta, so the two can be put together at the same time – most convenient. Wash, dry and halve the cherry tomatoes in advance; chop the skinned garlic cloves and fry them gently in the olive oil in advance, too, if it will save you time. This is a messily delicious main course to eat. Do remember to warn any of your guests who may be unaware that closed mussels* must not be eaten *because it means that they were dead when they were cooked. No one can tell how long a closed cooked mussel has been dead, so the safest thing is not to eat it! You do need a large pan or casserole for this.*

Serves 6

1.5 litres/2½ pints mussels
6 tsps large capers, plump, juicy and preferably
preserved in olive oil
6 tbsps olive oil
3 fat cloves of garlic, skinned and chopped
900 g/2 lb sweet cherry tomatoes, washed, dried
and cut in half
600 ml/1 pint vegetable stock (if you use a stock substitute,
I suggest Marigold powder)
½ tsp sugar
½ tsp salt, preferably Maldon
a good grinding of black pepper
375–450 g/12 oz–1 lb spaghetti
a handful of basil leaves, torn into bits

If the mussels have been picked from rocks, scrub them to remove any wisps of seaweed; this won't be necessary if they are farmed mussels. If the capers have been preserved in brine, drain and rinse

Spaghetti with mussels, tomatoes and capers

them well, under running cold water, and pat them dry with kitchen paper – this removes much of the harsh, vinegary brine taste.

Heat 3 tbsps olive oil in a very large pan which has a lid. Fry the chopped garlic over moderate heat – so as not to burn the garlic – for half a minute or so, then add the halved cherry tomatoes, Stir all around and let the tomatoes cook for a minute before adding the stock. Add the capers, sugar, salt and pepper, and the mussels. Clamp the lid on the pan and cook for 10 minutes.

Meanwhile, heat water to boiling point in another large saucepan. Add the spaghetti (how much you use depends on the ages and therefore – usually – the appetites of those who will eat this) and, when the water boils again, simmer for 7 minutes. Drain well, put the drained spaghetti back in the pan, add the remaining 3 table-spoons of olive oil and mix it in well – this prevents the pasta sticking together. Fork spaghetti on to each of six warmed soup plates and ladle the mussels on top of each serving, digging down with the ladle to scoop up the garlicky tomato and caper broth. Sprinkle with the torn basil leaves and serve.

Grilled plaice with red pepper, chive and parsley dressing

This makes the most of plaice, a fish I love. Plaice is a very light white fish – as opposed to more sturdy fish such as cod, hake, halibut, turbot and skate. This is such a convenient main course, because the red pepper and chive dressing can be made a couple of days in advance, then reheated to spoon over the fish once it has grilled. I like this served with very well mashed potatoes and with stir-fried sugarsnap peas with a splash of soya sauce and garlic.

Serves 6

6 plaice, each about 150–175 g/ 5–6 oz in weight
6 tsps olive oil
½ lime
a pinch of salt
a good grinding of black pepper

4 red peppers, cut in half, seeds removed   *For the dressing*
and the peppers diced small
6 tbsps olive oil
juice of ½ lime, squeezed into the dressing
½ tsp salt, preferably Maldon
a good grinding of black pepper
2 tbsps chopped parsley and snipped chives, mixed

First make the dressing. Mix the diced red peppers with the olive oil and spread them over a baking tray. Roast them in a hot oven, 220°C/420°F/gas mark 7 (top-right oven in an Aga), for 20 minutes. Then shuffle them around on the baking sheet and continue to roast them for a further 15–20 minutes. Take them from the oven. Scoop the contents of the baking sheet into a bowl, including all the olive oil, and stir in the squeezed lime juice, salt, pepper, chopped parsley

Grilled plaice with red pepper, chive and parsley dressing

and snipped chives. (You can make this several days in advance if you like. If you do, don't add the parsley and chives until you need the dressing, then reheat it gently in a saucepan).

To cook the fish, put a piece of foil over the grill pan. Cook the plaice in relays according to how many you can fit on the grill pan at one time. Have a large dish warmed to receive the plaice as they are cooked.

On each raw fish, smear a teaspoon of olive oil, a squeeze of lime juice, salt and pepper. Grill the fish under a hot grill, watching them, for about 45–60 seconds. Lift them carefully from the grill pan on to the pre-warmed dish, and spoon the dressing over each cooked plaice.

Prawn, roast asparagus and quails' egg salad with crispy bacon and herb dressing

This can be made only during the British asparagus season. I love roasting asparagus – we eat it as often as we can during its season. Imported asparagus is so very dreary in comparison to British-grown asparagus. The combination of roast asparagus, cooled, with prawns and quails' eggs in this main course salad dish is delicious, even if this is a composed recipe, requiring no actual cooking skills – itself a recommendation! The herb dressing is so simple, but it does make all the difference to this salad, and the crispy bacon is far more than just a garnish: it is everything I feel that a garnish should be – an integral part of the whole dish.

If possible, let the prawns be langoustines, but really they can be any type of prawn you choose – only please don't let them be those awful small pink prawns which can only be bought frozen and which, I am quite sure, are manufactured and owe nothing to nature!

Serves 6

675 g/1½ lb asparagus spears
olive oil
flaky salt, preferably Maldon
18 quails' eggs (3 per person)
450 g/1lb prawns
12 rashers smoked streaky bacon, grilled till crisp
then broken into bits

150ml/¼ pint olive oil *For the dressing*
½ tsp salt
a good grinding of black pepper
½ tsp caster sugar
1 tbsp lemon juice
2 tbsps chopped parsley and snipped chives, mixed

Prawn, roast asparagus and quails' egg salad with crispy bacon and herb dressing

Snap each asparagus spear – they will snap where the tough part begins; throw away the lower (tough) part of each spear. Put the trimmed spears on a baking sheet and brush the asparagus with olive oil. Sprinkle with flaky salt – Maldon is the salt I use – and roast the asparagus in a hot oven, 220°C/450°F/gas mark 7 (roasting oven in an Aga), for 15–20 minutes. Take the baking tray out of the oven and cool the roast asparagus.

Boil the quails' eggs for 3 minutes, then cool them under cold running water, shell them and cut each egg in half lengthways.

Mix together all the dressing ingredients in a screw-topped jar. Shake the jar vigorously to mix the ingredients thoroughly. Assemble the main course by arranging the prawns and asparagus on a large platter (ashet). Arrange the shelled and halved quails' eggs around and scatter the bits of crispy bacon over the lot. Shake the dressing and drizzle it over the whole thing. Serve with warm bread or rolls.

Razor fish in oatmeal with bacon

On the occasions when razor fish are available, I find myself being asked what to do with them. Razor fish are delicious and rare, but easily ruined by overcooking. This renders them tough and chewy. I like them best cooked like this. For this dish, I prefer to use streaky bacon, and smoked for my taste. I buy dry-cured bacon, which is a world apart from the standard bacon in most large retail outlets.

If you find pinhead oatmeal difficult to get, try a health-food shop. They are a wonderful source of ingredients that supermarkets often think not worth stocking. Pinhead oatmeal makes a perfect and delicious coating for all sorts of foods, from razor fish to all other types of filleted fish, and for chicken, too. But oatmeal of any sort relies on salt to bring out its taste.

Serves 6

2 razor fish per person (or more, if you have them!)
1 large egg, beaten, on a plate
225 g/8 oz pinhead oatmeal
1 tsp salt, preferably Maldon
a good grinding of black pepper
24 rashers of smoked streaky bacon,
or **12 rashers of back bacon if you prefer**
olive oil (optional)

Dip each razor fish in beaten egg, then in the pinhead oatmeal mixed with salt and pepper. Lay them on a baking tray which you first line with baking parchment.

Grill the bacon till crisp, and pour the fat from the bacon into a large sauté pan. You may need to top this up with olive oil. Fry the coated razor fish in the hot oil and fat for 30 seconds. Turn the fish and cook for a further 30 seconds on the other side, then remove them to a warm serving plate.

Hot-smoked salmon, pink grapefruit and chicory salad, with chive and horseradish dressing

This is a filling main course for a warm day. If you can't get chicory, try using Chinese leaves instead, or any crisp leaf. I love the slight bitterness of chicory as well as its crisp, juicy texture. The combination of pink grapefruit, smoked fish, horseradish and chives is very good. Steamed new potatoes are the perfect accompaniment to this salad, or warmed bread or rolls.

Serves 6

4 heads of chicory, the ends cut off and the leaves pulled apart
3 pink grapefruit (or ruby or red – they are all much the same thing)
900 g/2 lb hot-smoked salmon, the fish flaked from the skin into a bowl

For the dressing 6 tbsps olive oil
3 tsps balsamic vinegar
½ tsp salt, preferably Maldon
a good grinding of black pepper
1 tsp creamy horseradish (not a harsh vinegary brand)
2 tbsps snipped chives

Arrange the chicory leaves around a large serving plate. With a sharp serrated knife slice the skin and pith from the grapefruit, then slice in between the membrane of each segment, and add the pithless segments to the flaked salmon in the bowl. As you slice, add any juice which seeps from the fruit to the bowl, too.

Combine all the dressing ingredients, mixing thoroughly. Stir the dressing into the salmon and grapefruit segments – try not to break up the segments more than you can help as you mix in the dressing. Heap the salmon and grapefruit onto the serving plate, with the chicory leaves surrounding.

main courses for family and friends

Salmon quenelles

This recipe, and that for Smoked and Fresh Haddock Quenelles on pages 115–16, have both previously appeared in my book Entertaining Solo, *but I make no apology – they are so delicious and so easy! The mixture can be made up to a day in advance, and the quenelles will keep warm in their sauce for 30–40 minutes.*

Serves 6

675 g/1½ lb salmon, filleted, preferably organically farmed
2 anchovy fillets, drained of their oil
1 large egg
2 egg whites
300 ml/½ pint double cream
½ tsp Tabasco
a good grinding of black pepper
a grating of nutmeg
stock, made from water and Marigold vegetable
stock powder (see below)

For the tomato sauce

50 g/2 oz butter
1 red onion, skinned and chopped
4 ripe vine tomatoes, skinned, seeded and chopped
juice of 1 lemon
300 ml/½ pint double cream
½ tsp salt
a good grinding of black pepper

Put the salmon and anchovies into a food processor and add the egg, the egg whites, the cream and Tabasco, pepper and nutmeg. Whiz till smooth. Scrape the mixture into a bowl, cover, and put the bowl into the fridge for 3–4 hours or overnight.

Heat stock to a depth of 6–7.5 cm/2½–3 inches in a wide saucepan. When it has reached a fast boil, with two tablespoons form neat and even oval egg shapes of the fish mixture and slip them

Salmon quenelles

into the boiling stock. Poach them for 5 minutes, turning them over during that time. Butter an ovenproof dish, lift the poached quenelles from the stock with a slotted spoon and put them into the buttered dish.

To make the sauce, melt the butter in a saucepan and sauté the chopped red onion until very soft. Add the chopped tomatoes, lemon juice and cream. Simmer for 2 minutes, stirring. Take the pan off the heat, whiz the contents in a blender or processor, return to the pan and season with salt and pepper. Pour this sauce over the finished quenelles in their ovenproof dish. Cover the dish and keep it warm until you are ready to serve. (The chive cream sauce on page 115 is suitable for the salmon quenelles as well as the smoked haddock ones, but the creamy tomato sauce is a delicious alternative to serve over the salmon dish.)

main courses for family and friends

Barbecued salmon

I think this makes the salmon taste delicious. I like to serve it with mayon-naise, and how I flavour the mayonnaise depends on how I feel on the day, though usually I opt for the Cucumber and Dill Mayonnaise on page 254. But I always make a tomato and caper salad, with lemon (or lime) vinaigrette (see next page), and steamed new potatoes to eat with the salmon. Simple food, really, but nothing could be better.

Serves 6

**1.2 kg/2½ lb filleted organically farmed salmon, the skin left
on the fish
2 tbsps olive oil
lots of black pepper
1 lemon, washed well to remove preservative,
dried and sliced into 5–6 slices
75 g/3 oz parsley**

Lay a large sheet of foil on a work surface and put the salmon on this, skin-side down. Rub olive oil into the fish, grind lots of black pepper over, lay the lemon slices on the fish and strew the parsley over all. Seal the foil – like a Cornish pasty, scrimping it up in the middle. Slash the foil in several places with the point of a sharp knife – this allows the flavour of the glowing coals to permeate the fish.

Light the barbecue in plenty of time to allow the coals to burn up through flaming red to a white heat. Put the foil parcel on the coals and leave for 20 minutes. Then open the foil and, with two forks, prise apart the thickest bit of fish to check that it falls in succulent flakes. If it is still too undercooked for your liking, seal together the foil and leave the parcel to continue cooking on the coals.

Serve, with mayonnaise and a tomato and caper salad (see next page).

Tomato and caper salad

Serves 6

900 g/2 lb cherry tomatoes, washed well,
    dried and halved
4 tsps best-quality capers, plump and preferably
    preserved in olive oil

For the dressing   finely grated rind of 1 lemon, well washed to remove
    preservative and dried before grating
½ tsp salt, preferably Maldon
a good grinding of black pepper
½ tsp caster sugar
1 tsp Dijon mustard
150 ml/¼ pint olive oil
2 tsps balsamic vinegar
2 tbsps chopped parsley and snipped chives, mixed

Mix together all the dressing ingredients. Put the halved cherry tomatoes and the capers into a bowl, and mix the dressing in thoroughly.

main courses for family and friends

Salmon and dill cream tart

I see from my first fish book that I make this tart differently now from how I used to make it twenty-two years ago. Even then, I had realized that it is necessary to use raw salmon, never cooked. Twice-cooked salmon is so dry and tasteless that it isn't even redeemed by the lovely pastry and the creamy dill filling surrounding it. It goes without saying that the salmon used must only be organically farmed or wild, if you can get it. The Parmesan in the pastry is slight of taste – not much is used – but it makes all the difference.

This dish needs only a good mixed-leaf salad to accompany it, dressed with a mustardy vinaigrette.

Serves 6

110 g/4 oz butter cut in bits, hard from the fridge *For the pastry*
50 g/2 oz grated Parmesan cheese
175 g/6 oz plain flour
1 tsp icing sugar
lots of black pepper

675 g/1½ lb salmon, filleted but left in one piece (i.e. not sliced) *For the filling*
2 large eggs
2 egg yolks
300 ml/½ pint single cream
a pinch of salt
a good grinding of black pepper
a grating of nutmeg
25 g/1 oz dill, torn into bits

Put the ingredients for the pastry into a food processor and whiz to the texture of fine crumbs. Press this mixture firmly around the sides and base of a flan dish measuring 22 cm/9 inches in diameter, and about 5 cm/2 inches deep. Put the dish into the fridge for at least

Salmon and dill cream tart

1 hour, then bake it in a moderate oven, 180°C/350°F/gas mark 4 (bottom-right oven in a four-door Aga), for 20 minutes, or until the pastry is pale golden in colour and just beginning to shrink in from the sides. If, as often happens, the pastry seems to slip a bit down the sides, scrape it back into place with a metal spoon and bake for a further couple of minutes to 'set' the pastry. But set the timer! Let the cooked pastry cool before filling it.

Cut the salmon into chunks about 2.5 cm/1 inch in size, and put them over the base of the cooled pastry.

In a bowl, beat together the eggs and yolks, then beat in the cream. Mix very well. Season with a pinch of salt, the pepper and nutmeg, and mix in the torn dill. Pour this over the salmon in the pastry, easing the filling between the pieces of fish. Carefully put the pastry case and its filling into a moderate oven, the same as for baking the pastry, and bake until the filling is set in the centre – the last part to set. Gently shake the flan dish to check that the filling no longer wobbles. The baking should take about 25 minutes – maybe a bit longer. Check that it doesn't overcook. Take it out of the oven, and serve the tart warm.

main courses for family and friends

Roast tomato and shallot risotto with baked salmon

This is a dish where taste and convenience come together. The tomatoes can be roasted a day ahead of making the risotto, if that is more convenient for you. The tomatoes I use for this are sweet cherry tomatoes, washed and halved before roasting. The salmon must be organically farmed, or wild, and it takes barely 5 minutes to cook. If you like, a mixed-leaf salad, or wilted spinach with butter and nutmeg, would be an ideal accompaniment to the risotto and salmon, for both colour and flavour.

Serves 6

6 pieces of salmon, each weighing about 175 g/6 oz
6 tsps olive oil

900 g/2 lb cherry tomatoes, washed, dried and cut in half *For the risotto*
3 tbsps olive oil
1 tsp flaky salt, preferably Maldon
4 tbsps olive oil
4 large, or 8 small, banana or torpedo shallots, with violet-tinted flesh, skinned and diced finely
450 g/1 lb risotto rice, either arborio or carnaroli
150 ml/¼ pint fairly dry white wine
½ tsp dried chilli flakes (optional, but I always add them)
1.5 litres/2½ pints chicken or vegetable stock
finely grated rind of 1 lemon, well washed to remove preservative and dried before grating
a good grinding of black pepper
2 tbsps chopped parsley and snipped chives, mixed

Roast tomato and shallot risotto with baked salmon

To make the risotto, mix the halved cherry tomatoes very well with the 3 tablespoons of olive oil and the teaspoon of salt. Spread them on a baking tray or roasting tin (lined, if you like, with a sheet of baking parchment) and roast them in a slow oven, 140°C/250°F/gas ½ (top-left oven in a four-door Aga),for 2–2½ hours. Don't be tempted to roast them in a hotter oven because then they seep juice and roast and swim in the juice at the same time.

In a large sauté pan, heat the 4 tablespoons of olive oil and fry the diced shallots in the oil for several minutes until the shallots are quite soft and just beginning to turn colour at the edges. Stir in the rice, and cook for several minutes, stirring, so that each grain of rice is coated with oil and shallot. Then add the white wine and chilli flakes, and stir well, letting the wine bubble and evaporate before pouring in a small amount of the stock. Stir from time to time, and let the stock simmer and evaporate as the rice absorbs it, then add more stock, continuing until all the stock is used up. The risotto should be fairly sloppy and not at all stiff. Cook it gently and not over fierce heat. Lastly, add the lemon rind, pepper, slow-roast tomatoes and, just before serving, the chopped mixed parsley and chives.

Feel each piece of fish and remove any bones you encounter. To cook the salmon, lay a sheet of baking parchment on a baking tray and put the pieces of salmon on this. Put a teaspoon of olive oil on each piece of fish, cover with a second sheet of parchment and bake in a hot oven, 220°C/420°F/gas mark 7 (roasting oven in an Aga), for 5–7 minutes. Carefully stick a knife into the thickest bit of a piece of salmon to see if it is cooked – you can tell if it looks raw still; if it does, cover with paper and roast for a further 3–4 minutes.

Spoon the risotto on to six warmed plates and lay a piece of baked salmon on top of each serving of risotto.

main courses for family and friends

Skate

Of all fish, skate is my favourite, bar none. Skate differs from other white fish in several ways. It is best a couple of days old, rather than absolutely fresh. It comes in the form of 'wings', which are composed of ridges of cartilage, and the utterly delicious flesh is between the cartilage ribs. These long, succulent, slightly gelatinous strips are simply the best fish, which needs only the Brown Butter, Lemon and Caper Sauce on page 270 to accompany it. The skate wings should be simmered gently in a stock, correctly called a court bouillon.

Serves 6

2 skate wings, each weighing about 675 g/1½ lb

1.2 litres/2 pints water *For the stock*
1 tsp salt, preferably Maldon
2 tsps black peppercorns
1 carrot, well washed and thickly sliced
1 onion, skinned and quartered
2 celery sticks, washed and cut in half
a small handful of parsley stalks, crushed to release their flavour
2 bay leaves

Put the stock ingredients into a large saucepan and bring the water to the boil. Simmer gently for 5 minutes, then cool the stock completely.

To cook the skate, put the wings into a roasting tin and, through a sieve, strain the cold stock over the fish. Put the roasting tin into a moderate oven, 180°C/350°F/gas mark 4 (bottom-right oven in a four-door Aga), for 10 minutes, then cover the surface with baking

Skate

parchment and bake for a further 20–25 minutes, or until, when you lift out the roasting tin and gently prise between two ribs of cartilage with two forks, the fish lifts easily from between them. Serve, either cutting each wing in three – messy – or by forking the fish yourself and dividing it between six warmed plates. This is inelegant, but never mind – it is absolutely delicious. Serve with the Brown Butter, Lemon and Caper sauce (page 270), any green vegetable and either new or well-mashed potatoes.

Squid in chilli sauce provençale

This is such a low-calorie recipe, but one full of good tastes. Which type of chilli and how much you use depends on how much you love it – we are completely addicted as a family, but I am very aware of this so I tend to give quite modest amounts in written recipes. Increase the chilli if you choose.

Squid comes into our waters as they warm up, as the summer months progress. I love it, but it must be tender. By soaking squid in milk (the simplest of all marinades) you tenderize it. Be sure to dry it as best you can before cooking – I pat it dry with a wodge of kitchen paper. Serve this with anything you choose – for me that is boiled basmati rice or couscous, and a good leaf salad dressed with Dijon mustard vinaigrette.

Serves 6

900 g/2 lb squid, weighed when trimmed
milk to cover the squid
6 tbsps olive oil
2 medium-sized onions, skinned and diced finely
2 sticks of celery, trimmed of stringy bits and sliced thinly
2 fat cloves of garlic, skinned and chopped finely
3 tins of chopped tomatoes, each weighing 400 g/15 oz
½ tsp dried chilli flakes
½ tsp sugar (to counteract bitterness from the tomato seeds)
½ tsp salt
a good grinding of black pepper
1 tbsp chopped parsley
about 25 g/1 oz basil leaves, torn into bits

Slice the squid into rings and the tentacles into 5-cm/2-inch lengths. Put the prepared squid into a dish and cover it with milk. Cover the dish with clingfilm and leave it in the fridge for several hours or overnight. Before cooking, drain the squid through a sieve (or colander), throwing away the milk – sorry, but really it isn't good for anything. Pat the squid dry, in the sieve or colander, as best you can.

Squid in chilli sauce provençale

To make the sauce, heat 4 tablespoons of the olive oil in a large saucepan. Fry the diced onion and sliced celery for several minutes, stirring from time to time to make sure that the onions and celery cook evenly. Then stir in the chopped garlic and the contents of the tins of tomatoes, stirring all together very well. Stir in the chilli, sugar, salt and pepper and let the sauce simmer gently for 5 minutes.

In a sauté pan, heat the remainder of the olive oil and, over a fairly high heat, stir-fry the squid for 2 minutes. Then scoop the contents of the sauté pan into the simmering sauce. Cook for a minute, and then stir in the torn basil and chopped parsley just before serving. Try not to leave the cooked squid in the hot sauce for very long, because the longer it sits in the heat the more it will toughen.

main courses for family and friends

Trout baked in cream with toasted almonds

We eat very little freshwater fish. I have just read a piece in the Spectator *on the delights of eating perch. I can only think that the writer lives a long way from the sea. We are spoilt, living surrounded by sea here in Skye and eating as much fish as we do, but for me there is simply no contest between sea fish and freshwater fish, except for trout and salmon. I love both. Salmon really are both, the extraordinary fish that they are – really miracles of nature, being both sea and freshwater fish. But trout are entirely freshwater living (unless they are that rare delicacy, a sea trout, now sadly scarce) and they can be brown trout, or the more usually found rainbow trout. The trout we buy from fishmongers and supermarket fish counters are farmed. Try to buy organically farmed trout. This recipe and the following one are for all types of trout.*

Serves 6

6 trout
110 g/4 oz flaked almonds
3 tbsps olive oil
450 ml/¾ pint double cream
1 tsp lemon juice
½ tsp salt
a good grinding of black pepper
2 tbsps snipped chives (use scissors and snip them finely: it looks better)

When you buy your trout they will be cleaned. If you catch your own, slit them down the length of the fish, and, under running cold water, remove all their innards – this takes seconds. Pat each trout dry on kitchen paper. Leave the heads on.

In a large sauté pan, dry-fry the flaked almonds (no oil or butter) over a moderately high heat, shaking the pan from time to time until

Trout baked in cream with toasted almonds

the flaked almonds are turning light brown. Scoop them from the pan into a bowl. Add the olive oil to the same sauté pan – no need to wash it: the flavour of toasted almonds is what we want – and fry each trout for 1 minute on each side. You will probably be able to fry 3 trout at a time. As they cook, remove them to a large, warm serving dish.

When the trout are cooked, put the toasted flaked almonds back in the sauté pan, add the double cream and let the cream bubble. Simmer for a minute, then stir in the teaspoon of lemon juice, the salt, pepper and snipped chives. Pour and spoon this over the trout on their serving dish. Somehow the taste of toasted almonds is very good with the fish.

I like to serve new potatoes with mint if in season – or mashed potatoes if not – and a green vegetable such as courgettes stir-fried in olive oil with garlic.

Butter and parsley fried trout with lemon

This could not be simpler, but it tastes very good. This is how we eat trout in the guesthouse in the remote village in Austria, where our eldest daughter, Alexandra, lives with her family.

The amount of parsley used in this recipe sounds a lot, and it is, but a depth of parsley is a main feature of the dish.

Serves 6

175 g/6 oz butter (I use Lurpak)
6 trout, cleaned (see page 15) and heads left on
6 tbsps chopped parsley
½ tsp salt
a good grinding of black pepper
1 lemon, cut in half, then each half cut into 3 wedges

Melt half the amount of butter in a large sauté pan and fry 3 trout for 1 minute before turning them over to fry for another minute on their other side. As they are cooked, remove them to a warm serving dish. Before frying the next 3 trout, melt the remaining butter in the sauté pan. Repeat the cooking process with the remaining 3 trout. When they are cooked, put them on the warm plate too.

Then stir the chopped parsley into the buttery juices in the sauté pan and, over a moderately high heat, fry the parsley, mixing in the salt and pepper. Cook for 1–2 minutes, stirring, then put a spoonful of the butter-fried parsley down each trout, and serve accompanied by the lemon wedges. So easy, and so good!

Tuna burgers

I call these 'burgers', aware that I deeply dislike the word, but I find myself unable to describe them otherwise. Both rissoles and fishcakes are made with cooked fish, so those words are out, and there doesn't seem to be an alternative! So burgers they remain.

These are made from very finely chopped raw tuna – or any other meaty-fleshed fish, like swordfish, for instance. You can, and I usually do, pulverize the fish in a food processor. Don't form the tuna mixture into cakes which are too deep, otherwise they will be too raw in the middle. They are very good with the Avocado Salsa (see page 260) and a leaf salad – young spinach mixed with watercress is a good combination of leaf tastes. But tuna burgers are filling, so whether you serve them on their own or in a buttered bun is up to you and will depend on the appetites of those who will be eating this convenient (they can be made a day in advance of cooking) and delicious variation on a fishcake.

Serves 6

1.2 kg/2½ lb tuna, cut into small bits (this makes processing easier)
½ small red onion, skinned and chopped
1 tbsp strong soy sauce
a good grinding of black pepper
2 tbsps chopped coriander
olive oil, for frying the burgers

Put the cut-up fish into the food processor with the chopped red onion, soy sauce, pepper and coriander. Whiz till the mixture is pulverized but not puréed. Scrape the mixture from the processor into a bowl. With wetted hands form the mixture into 12 even-sized balls, flattening each. If you do this in advance of cooking them, line a tray with a sheet of baking parchment and put the burgers on this. Cover them with a second sheet of baking parchment and cover the

whole with clingfilm. Put the tray and its contents into the fridge until you are ready to cook.

Heat olive oil to a depth of 0.5 cm/¼ inch in a sauté pan and fry the burgers. Once you have put them into the sauté pan in the hot oil, leave them alone: don't be tempted to push them around in the pan with the spatula or fish slice. Let them fry for 1½ minutes or so before turning them over to cook for the same length of time on the other side. Fry them for less time if you like the fish to be more underdone. Lift them on to a warmed dish lined with kitchen paper, to absorb excess oil, and keep the burgers warm until you are ready to eat them. They will keep warm without deteriorating for about 20 minutes in a low-temperature oven.

Marinated tuna, seared with lime, coriander, garlic and ginger

The fish is marinated in a mixture which is then poured into the sauté pan around the seared fish, with coriander added to it. It is easy these days to buy fresh tuna, which I love. Tuna, as you will most probably know, is a meaty-textured fish, lending itself to strong flavours, as in this marinade-cum-sauce. But the absolute essential is that the tuna is fresh and never frozen – you can always tell tuna which has been frozen. This is good with very well mashed potatoes and sugarsnap peas, stir-fried with garlic and ginger in olive oil, which echo the tastes of the marinated tuna.

Ask the fishmonger to slice the tuna thinly for you, or it is easy to do it yourself, provided you have a good, sharp knife – the most time-saving gadget in any kitchen.

Serves 6

1.2 kg/2½ lb tuna, sliced fairly thin, about 0.5-cm/¼-inch thickness

For the marinade
300 ml/½ pint olive oil
1–2 cloves of garlic, skinned and chopped finely
5-cm/2-inch piece of root ginger, skin pared off and the
**   ginger coarsely grated**
2 tbsps strong soy sauce
juice and finely grated rind of 2 limes, washed well to
**   remove preservative and dried before grating**
75 g/3 oz coriander, chopped quite coarsely

Heat the olive oil and, over gentle heat, cook the garlic and ginger for 2–3 minutes. Take the pan off the heat, and let the garlic, ginger and oil cool completely. Then mix in the soy sauce, lime rinds and juices.

Put the sliced tuna in a wide, shallow dish. Pour the cooled olive oil mixture from the sauté pan over the slices of raw tuna, cover the dish and leave for 2–3 hours.

main courses for family and friends

When you are ready to cook them, lift the slices of tuna from their marinade, letting them drip excess marinade back into the dish, and put the drained slices of fish on to another tray or dish. Heat a dry sauté pan over a moderately high heat. Have ready warming a wide, shallow ovenproof dish. Sear the drained slices of tuna in the very hot, dry pan, allowing a few seconds' cooking on each side (literally, 5–6 seconds on each side is enough, providing the pan is hot) and as the slices of fish cook lift them on to the warmed serving dish. When all the fish is cooked, pour the marinade and coriander into the sauté pan and bubble this for 1–2 minutes, then pour it over the cooked tuna slices. Serve.

Jerusalem artichokes and fish stir-fried with ginger and spring onions

This is easy and quick, bar the peeling of the artichokes. The season for Jerusalem artichokes now extends for about seven months, from the end of November right through to June, so we can make the most of this most delicious of all root vegetables, which has a peculiarly wonderful affinity with fish and shellfish of all types. A firm-fleshed fish is essential for this recipe, and monkfish is top of the list for that, but you can use hake or cod instead. I like boiled basmati rice and roast courgettes with this, but any other green vegetable would do.

If you prepare the artichokes in advance, toss the slivers in lemon juice (about 4 tablespoons) to prevent them discolouring.

Serves 6

6 tbsps olive oil
approx. 5 cm/2 inches fresh root ginger, skin pared off and
    the ginger chopped or grated coarsely
450 g/1 lb Jerusalem artichokes, weighed when peeled,
    and sliced into fine slivers
12 spring onions, trimmed and sliced diagonally into pieces
    about 2.5 cm/1 inch in length
900 g/2 lb firm-fleshed white fish, membrane trimmed off and
    the fish cut into 2.5-cm/1-inch pieces
½ tsp salt
a good grinding of black pepper

Heat the olive oil in a large casserole or sauté pan. Add the ginger, slivers of artichoke and the spring onions, and stir-fry all together over a fairly high heat for 7–10 minutes. Then add the pieces of fish to the pan and continue to stir-fry for a further 5 minutes, or until the pieces of fish turn opaque. Season with salt and pepper.

This will keep warm in a low heat, in a warmed ovenproof dish covered loosely with foil, for up to 30 minutes.

main courses for family and friends

Sri Lankan fish curry

Our family love spiced foods of all types, but it is only in the past fifteen years that I have been using fish in a curry. For this recipe you can use any firm-fleshed fish – tuna, or monkfish, marlin (if you live where you can get it), salmon, hake, cod, ling, or even a mixture. I have been told that if fish is marinated in coconut milk for a minimum of 2 hours, it holds its shape when cooked, even if it is a fish – like cod – which usually falls into flakes if it is as fresh as it should be. I am not convinced about this! But these combined tastes are utterly delicious, and, whichever fish you use, if you, too, like spicy, chilli-containing food, then I urge you to try this.

Serves 6

1.2 kg/2½ lb firm-fleshed fish
2 x 400 ml (15 fl oz) tins coconut milk (total weight 400 g/15 oz)
2 tbsps olive oil
2 onions, skinned and finely diced
1–2 fat cloves of garlic, skinned and chopped finely
about 5 cm/2 inches fresh root ginger, skin pared off
and the ginger chopped finely or grated
1 stick of lemongrass, bashed with a rolling pin
1 level tsp dried chilli flakes
2 level tsps cornflour (I seldom use this in savoury recipes,
but it belongs here)
juice and finely grated rind of 2 limes, washed well
to remove preservative and dried before grating
300 ml/½ pint double cream
75 g/3 oz coriander, chopped, but not finely
½ teaspoon salt, preferably Maldon
a good grinding of black pepper

Sri Lankan fish curry

Put the fish on a board and feel it all over, pulling out or cutting out any bones that you find. Then cut the fish into pieces about 4 cm/ 2 inches in size. Put the cut-up fish into a bowl and pour on the contents of the cans of coconut milk. Leave for 2 hours or so, covered, in the fridge.

In a large casserole, heat the olive oil and fry the finely diced onion for several minutes, stirring occasionally to prevent it overcooking, until it is soft and transparent-looking. Then stir in the garlic and ginger, and the bashed stick of lemongrass. Cook all together over a moderate heat – not too hot. Stir in the dried chilli flakes, and the cornflour, stirring all together very well. Then pour in the coconut milk marinade from the fish, and stir until the mixture bubbles gently. Stir in the lime rinds and the pieces of fish and cook at a gentle simmer for 5 minutes. The pieces of fish will then be just cooked through. Stir in the lime juice, double cream and the chopped coriander and season with salt and pepper. Serve, with boiled basmati rice and a mixed-leaf salad.

This will keep warm satisfactorily for up to 1 hour.

Fish Florentine

You can use any firm-fleshed white fish in this – cod, hake, megrim, ling, whiting, to list just five – but not fish like plaice, which is too soft. The spinach, well seasoned with salt, pepper and nutmeg, with the fish in pieces on top and then the covering of cheese sauce is an excellent combination of tastes.

The cheese sauce can be dull, either through lack of cheese or, odd though it may sound, through too much cheese, in which case the sauce is almost glue-like through fat content. What is needed is judicious seasoning to enhance the cheese content: this is far more effective and much, much nicer to eat than just using more and more cheese. I promise the dash of Tabasco won't make the sauce too fiery hot – it just contributes to the whole flavour. And a thin crust of melted cheese on top – for me, this is grated Parmesan. The only thing required to accompany this main course is either new potatoes in season, baked jacket potatoes or warm bread.

Serves 6

900 g/2 lb young spinach – 4 bags x 225 g/8 oz each
2 tbsps olive oil
½ tsp salt
a good grinding of black pepper
a grating of nutmeg
1.2 kg/2½ lb firm-fleshed white fish

50 g/2 oz butter   *For the cheese*
50 g/2 oz flour   *sauce*
750 ml/1¼ pints milk
110 g/4 oz Cheddar cheese, grated
a dash of Tabasco
1 heaped tsp best-quality Dijon mustard,
or 2 tsps balsamic vinegar
a pinch of salt
a grinding of black pepper
a pinch of nutmeg
75 g/3 oz grated Parmesan, for scattering over the surface

Fish Florentine

The amount of spinach looks huge, but you will know that as soon as it heats, spinach wilts down and also seeps liquid – it is mostly water in its composition. So, briefly steam the spinach, in relays, and after barely a minute for each batch put it on to a plastic tray to cool. Squeeze excess liquid from the wilted spinach, turn it into a bowl and chop it – scissors are best for this. At the same time add the olive oil, salt, pepper and nutmeg, mixing all into the chopped spinach thoroughly. Put the spinach over the base of an ovenproof dish that is sufficiently big to hold the spinach when covered with the fish and sauce.

Feel the fish on a board, removing all bones encountered, then line a baking tray with baking parchment, put the de-boned fish on this, in either 6 pieces or in a layer of bite-sized chunks, about 4 cm/1½ inches in size, cover with a second sheet of baking parchment and steam-bake the fish in a moderate oven, 180°C/350°F/gas mark 4 (bottom-right oven in a four-door Aga), for 10 minutes. The fish won't be cooked through – it isn't meant to be; it will complete its cooking time as the finished Florentine bakes. Put the pieces of partially cooked fish on to the spinach.

Make the sauce by melting the butter in a saucepan and stirring in the flour. Let this cook for a couple of minutes before gradually adding the milk, stirring continuously until the sauce boils. Let the sauce bubble gently for a minute then draw the pan off the heat and stir in the grated Cheddar cheese, Tabasco, Dijon mustard (or balsamic vinegar), salt, pepper and nutmeg. Mix well, until the cheese melts completely. Cool the sauce a bit before pouring it over the fish. Cover with the grated Parmesan cheese, and bake in a moderate oven, 180°C/350°F/gas mark 4 (bottom-right oven in a four-door Aga), for 30–35 minutes, or until the cheese has melted on the surface and forms a golden crust.

You can make the Florentine several hours in advance, but I find it is best made the day that it is to be eaten. However, the spinach can be prepared a day in advance, and the fish felt and de-boned. Keep both, covered, in the fridge until you are ready to complete the making of the dish.

main courses for family and friends

Smoked fish and spinach lasagne

You can use any type of smoked fish you like for this recipe, but most probably that will mean smoked haddock. I love smoked cod; if you can get it, I do urge you to try it. Smoked cod has fat juicy flakes of fish, and the bones are much easier to pull out than those in haddock, because they are larger. The combined flavours of smoked fish with cheese and spinach are, for me, sublime.

This is also a recipe after my own heart, where everything is in one dish – protein, starch (the lasagne) and vegetables (onions and spinach). I really think that any accompaniment is superfluous; the exception might be a mixed-leaf salad with a Dijon mustard vinaigrette.

You will notice that the sauce is very sloppy, but this is necessary because, as the lasagne bakes, the sheets of pasta absorb the excess liquid from the sauce. Too thick a sauce gives you a stodgy lasagne.

Serves 6

900 g/2 lb smoked fish
1.5 litres/2½ pints milk
50 g/2 oz butter and 2 tbsps olive oil
2 onions, skinned and neatly and finely diced
2 tbsps flour
1 tsp Dijon mustard
a good grinding of black pepper
a grating of nutmeg
450 g/1 lb young spinach leaves
175 g/6 oz grated cheese (Cheddar, or you could use
Gruyère, Lancashire or Parmesan)
12 sheets of green lasagne

Rub a large ovenproof dish, about 3.6-litre/6-pint pint capacity, with olive oil.

Put the fillets of fish on a board and feel them, cutting or pulling out any bones you discover. Cut the fish into pieces about 5 cm/ 2 inches in size. Put the pieces of fish into a large saucepan with the

Smoked fish and spinach lasagne

milk and, over a moderate heat, cook until the milk just begins to bubble. Take the pan off the heat and leave the fish to cool completely. As it does, it infuses the milk with its flavour. When cold, strain the milk into a measure jug and keep it to make into the sauce.

Meanwhile, melt the butter and heat it together with the olive oil in a saucepan. Add the diced onions and fry, stirring occasionally, for 4–5 minutes, or until they are completely transparent and soft. Stir in the flour, cook for a minute then gradually add the reserved milk, stirring continuously until the sauce boils. Draw the pan off the heat and stir in the Dijon mustard, pepper and nutmeg.

Wilt the spinach by cooking for 1 minute in 2 tablespoons boiling water with the lid on the saucepan. Drain and squeeze excess liquid from the spinach. Chop the wilted spinach – I use scissors for this. Stir the chopped spinach and half the grated cheese into the sauce. When it has cooled, stir in the pieces of fish. Spoon some of this mixture over the base of the ovenproof dish, cover with sheets of lasagne, and repeat, layering up both lasagne and sauce but ending with the sauce. You may have to break the lasagne sheets to fit the dish; don't worry. Scatter the remaining grated cheese over the surface and bake in a moderate oven, 180°C/350°F/gas mark 4 (bottom-right oven in a four-door Aga), for 40–45 minutes. Test to check that the pasta is cooked through by sticking a knife in the middle – it should feel quite soft.

You can prepare this several hours ahead of cooking, if it is more convenient for you. But do remember to take it from the fridge into room temperature at least 30 minutes before baking the lasagne.

Parsnip and smoked fish cakes

Mashed parsnips make a delicious alternative to the more usual mashed potato and smoked fish combination for fish cakes. Use any type of smoked fish you like, but this will most probably be smoked haddock. You can whiz the mashed parsnips in a food processor; unlike potatoes, they will not be rendered to the consistency of wallpaper glue.

Serves 6

900 g/2 lb parsnips, weighed when peeled
50 g/2 oz butter
½ tsp salt
a good grinding of black pepper
a grating of nutmeg
2 tbsps chopped parsley and snipped chives, mixed
900 g/2 lb smoked fish
300 ml/½ pint milk

2 large eggs, beaten, on a plate *For the fish cake*
175 g/6 oz sesame seeds mixed with 1 tsp salt *coating*

olive oil for frying

Cut the peeled parsnips into chunks and boil in salted water until they are tender. Drain them thoroughly and mash them with the butter, using a potato-masher. Alternatively, if you like to get a really smooth parsnip purée, whiz the mashed parsnips with the butter in a food processor, then scrape them into a bowl. Mix in salt, pepper and nutmeg and, when cooled, the parsley and chives.

Put the fish on a board, feel it thoroughly and either cut out or pull out any bones you encounter. Lay a sheet of baking parchment on a baking dish and put the boned smoked fish fillets on this. Cover with the milk – this is very little milk for the amount of fish, but it is just enough to keep the fish succulent as it cooks. Cover with a second sheet of baking parchment and bake in a moderate heat,

Parsnip and smoked fish cakes

180°C/350°F/gas mark 4 (bottom-right oven in a four-door Aga), for 20–25 minutes.

Take the tray out of the oven and cool, then flake the cooked fish into the bowl of parsnip purée and mix well – really, the only way to do this thoroughly is with your hand. Wet your hand to form the mixture into cakes. Make even-sized balls then flatten them, and dip each into the beaten egg then the salted sesame seeds. Put the coated fishcakes on to a plastic tray and, when you have made them all, cover with a sheet of baking parchment then with clingfilm and keep them in the fridge. These can be made a day ahead. They can be frozen, but not for much longer than 10–14 days. Thaw them for 2 hours at room temperature before frying.

Heat olive oil, just a covering over the base of a sauté pan, and when you put the fish cakes into the hot oil leave them alone for a couple of minutes before turning them over to fry on the other side. Do not be tempted to shuffle them around in the sauté pan, because they will break up if you do. Be warned!

These are good with stir-fried courgettes, which I like to slice to spaghetti-like thickness in a mandolin and cook with chopped garlic. Or serve them with mangetouts and, if you like, Tomato and Horseradish Cream (see page 257).

main courses for family and friends

Roast red pepper, chilli and tomato fish stew

This is one of those dishes so dear to my heart because the vegetables and fish are in one pot, needing only perhaps boiled basmati rice to go with them. The sauce and vegetable part can be done a day in advance, as can the fish preparation. Both must be kept in the fridge overnight and you need only reheat the vegetable sauce and add the pieces of fish to cook – maximum time 5 minutes.

Any firm-fleshed white fish – cod, halibut, ling, whiting, hake or megrim – is suitable for this recipe.

Serves 6

1.2 kg/2½ lb firm-fleshed white fish
4 red peppers
5 tbsps olive oil
3 red onions, skinned and sliced thinly
1–2 fat cloves of garlic, skinned and finely chopped
3 tins of chopped tomatoes, each weighing 400 g/15 oz
½ tsp dried chilli flakes
½ tsp salt, preferably Maldon
a good grinding of black pepper

Feel the fish on a board and remove any bones you encounter. Cut the fish into bite-size pieces, about 2.5 cm/1 inch in size.

Cut each pepper in half, scoop the seeds away and put the pepper halves, skin uppermost, under a hot grill until black blisters form. Transfer to a polythene bag for 10 minutes, then peel off the skins.

Heat the olive oil in a large casserole and fry the sliced onions until very soft. Then slice the skinned pepper halves into strips and add those to the onions in the casserole, as well as the chopped garlic. Cook all together for a minute before stirring in the contents of the tins of tomatoes. Add the chilli flakes, then season with salt and pepper and let the sauce bubble gently for 5 minutes – the sweetness of the peppers will counteract any slight bitterness from the tomato seeds. Add the pieces of fish, and simmer all together gently for 3–5 minutes. Serve.

Smoked fish and cheese soufflé

No one need be scared of soufflé-making. The tip that was given to me by my friend Charlotte Hunt, passed to her by her mother, Mrs Munro of Foulis, that a soufflé can be made in its entirety several hours before baking it, transformed my life – and the lives of all to whom I have passed on this invaluable knowledge over the years through cooking demonstrations. The finished uncooked soufflé must have clingfilm over the top of the dish, which is then removed before the soufflé is popped into the oven to cook. The only imperative with this and every soufflé is that it must be eaten as soon as it is taken out of the oven – a soufflé kept waiting, even for a few minutes, inexorably sinks and the sight is indeed a very sad one! A mixed-leaf salad, dressed with a mustardy vinaigrette, is the perfect accompaniment to this soufflé.

Serves 6

675 g/1½ lb smoked haddock
900 ml/1½ pints milk, for cooking the fish and making the sauce
75 g/3 oz butter
2 rounded tbsps flour
175 g/6 oz grated cheese
lots of freshly ground black pepper
a good grating of nutmeg
1 tsp Dijon mustard
6 large eggs, yolks separated from the whites,
the whites in a large bowl

Butter a fairly large soufflé dish, about 25 cm/10 inches in diameter.

Feel the smoked haddock, on a board, and remove any bones by cutting either side of the thin line of fine bones and throwing away the strip of flesh and bones. Cut up the fish into pieces about 2 cm/1 inch in size and put the fish into a saucepan. Cover the fish with the milk and, over a moderate heat, bring the milk to a simmering point. Then take the pan off the heat and let the contents cool completely.

Strain off the milk into a jug, measure out 750 ml/1¼ pints of it for the sauce and throw away the very small amount left.

Melt the butter in a large, non-stick saucepan. Stir in the flour and let this cook for a couple of minutes before gradually adding the reserved strained fish milk, stirring all the time until the sauce boils.

Let the sauce bubble gently for a few minutes, then draw the pan off the heat and stir in the grated cheese, pepper, nutmeg and Dijon mustard, stirring till the cheese has melted completely. Beat in the egg yolks one by one and mix each in thoroughly before adding the next. Let the sauce stand for 10 minutes to cool down a bit. Put the egg whites in a large bowl, add a pinch of salt and, easiest done with a hand-held electric whisk, whisk them up till they are glossy and stiff. Fold the stiffly whisked whites through the cheese sauce, adding the cooked fish alternately with spoonfuls of the whites. Pour this mixture into the buttered soufflé dish, cover with clingfilm and leave for 3–4 or more hours until you are ready to cook the soufflé.

Remove the clingfilm. Bake the soufflé in a hot oven, 220°C/420°F/gas mark 7 (roasting oven in an Aga), for 35–40 minutes. The soufflé should still be a bit runny when you spoon into it. Serve immediately.

Fish pie

This is a dish which can be food for the gods, or it can be pretentiously and spectacularly dull. To make it pretentious and dull, you need add no smoked fish (to me a sin) and include those deadly small prawns which can only be bought frozen, are the pink of old ladies' knickers, and which taste of worse than nothing, which is cardboard! The sauce manages to taste of nothing, not even butter, and the flour won't have been cooked enough. When mashed potato covers such a fish pie it rounds off the blandness, and I am convinced that it is this sort of fish pie that gives British cooking a bad name.

Contrast such a dismal affair with a fish pie made with smoked fish – haddock, usually – where the sauce is made using the milk in which the fish has cooked and cooled, and is therefore infused with the smoked fish taste. I love to include a small amount of firm-fleshed white fish – cod, or, for a ritzy pie, halibut. I also love to fry smoked bacon (back bacon) in with the small amount of onion to start the pie; bacon has such an excellent affinity with fish and it makes the tastes within a fish pie even better. I use full-fat proper milk for the sauce – how can a good sauce not taste watered down if skimmed milk is used? Unless you add lots of cream and butter, which negates the skimmed-ness of the milk in the first place. I also like to add lots of chopped parsley to the sauce – it loses some of its bright, fresh colour in the heat, but it still retains lots of taste. And a good layer of finely grated Parmesan cheese over the surface of the mashed potatoes makes a crisp, golden crust.

It is important to feel the fish before cooking it, and to remove the bones your fingers will discover where your eyes can't see them. To be able to reassure your family that the fish pie is almost certainly bone free is a very good selling point to those wary of eating fish through fear of finding a bone in a mouthful. And if tomato ketchup is requested – I love it – then never take umbrage. My mother always did, thinking we implied that her fish pies lacked in taste. But they never did – I learnt how to make fish pie from her in the first place! I think the reason is that she doesn't like tomato ketchup herself! But the ketchup must be Heinz: no other is good enough.

This recipe can be made in advance by a day and kept, covered, in the fridge. I recently froze one whole surplus fish pie and ate it three weeks later, and I would never have known it had been frozen. So do freeze a fish pie, but for a limited number of weeks – I would say four maximum.

675 g/1½ lb smoked haddock
450 g/1 lb white fish – haddock or halibut, depending on the occasion
a blade of mace
a celery stick
½ onion, skin removed
1.2 litres/2 pints milk
75 g/3 oz butter
1 small onion, skinned and diced finely
3 rashers of smoked back bacon, preferably dry-cured
50 g/2 oz flour
lots of freshly ground black pepper
a grinding of nutmeg
2 heaped tbsps chopped parsley

1.3 kg/3 lb potatoes, weighed before peeling *For the potato*
50 g/2 oz butter *covering*
150 ml/¼ pint milk, warmed
½ tsp salt
a good grinding of black pepper
a grating of nutmeg
75 g/3 oz grated Parmesan cheese – or Cheddar, if you prefer

Feel the smoked fish, on a board, and cut either side of the row of tiny bones and throw this out – you waste very little fish, so don't worry. With bigger-boned fish it is easier to pull out bones individually, but not with haddock. Do the same with the white fish. Cut the fish into chunks about 2.5 cm/1 inch in size and put the fish into a saucepan with the mace, stick of celery broken in half and the half-onion. Pour in the milk and cook the fish over a moderate heat, letting the milk come to simmering point. Push the fish down into the milk, if the milk doesn't quite cover it. Then take the pan off the heat once simmering is reached, and leave the fish and milk to cool. Once cooled, strain off the milk and keep it for the sauce. Pick out and throw away the celery, onion and mace.

Fish pie

Melt the 75 g/3 oz butter in a large saucepan and fry the diced onion and bacon strips together for several minutes, until the onion is quite soft and transparent-looking. Then stir in the flour and let this cook for a couple of minutes before adding the strained milk gradually, stirring continuously. When the sauce boils, let it bubble gently for a minute, then draw the pan off the heat. Season with pepper and nutmeg, add the cooked pieces of fish, stir in the chopped parsley and pour this into an ovenproof dish. Leave to cool.

Meanwhile, peel the potatoes and cook in boiling water with a teaspoon of salt added to the water. When the potatoes are soft when stuck with a knife, drain off the cooking water and, shaking the pan over heat, steam off excess water. Take the pan off the heat and mash the potatoes well. Melt the butter in the milk, then with a wooden spoon beat the potatoes, adding the melted butter and milk. Season with salt, pepper and nutmeg, and cover the cold fish base with the mashed potatoes, forking the surface in lines. Cover with grated Parmesan or Cheddar. Reheat in a moderate oven, 180°C/350°F/gas mark 4 (bottom-right oven in a four-door Aga), for 35–40 minutes, or until the sauce is bubbling around under the edge of the potato and the cheese has melted over the surface, forming a golden-brown crust. Serve, with either a mixed-leaf salad, or with peas, or both.

Fish with leeks, apples and ginger

Use any firm-fleshed white fish for this, but best of all is monkfish, because that holds its shape when cooked, whereas other fish – cod, hake – tend to fall into large flakes if left in the heat for any length of time. The apples and ginger in this recipe are so good with the fish, and here is another example of fish and vegetables in one dish. New potatoes in season, or very well mashed potatoes, are good with this.

Serves 6

900 g/2 lb fish – monkfish, cod, hake, ling, megrim, for example

4 tbsps olive oil

6 leeks, washed, trimmed, and sliced diagonally into pieces about 5 cm/2 inches long

approx. 5-cm/2-inch piece of fresh root ginger, skin pared off and the ginger coarsely grated or chopped finely

6 good eating apples (*not* Golden Delicious!), cut in quarters, peeled, cored and sliced

12 fat cloves of garlic, skinned and chopped finely

300 ml/½ pint dry cider

2 tbsps dark soy sauce

lots of black pepper

Feel the fish on a board, removing any skin and all bones. Cut the fish into pieces about 4 cm/1½ inches in size. You can do this a day in advance, but keep the prepared fish in a covered bowl in the fridge overnight.

Heat the olive oil in a large sauté pan and add the leeks and ginger to the oil. Over a moderate heat, cook the leeks, stirring them around in the pan so that they cook evenly, then add the apple slices and chopped garlic. Cook, stirring from time to time, for 2–3 minutes, then add the cider and soy sauce. Let this mixture simmer gently for 2–3 minutes. Season with black pepper, mix it in, then add the pieces of fish to the gently simmering contents of the sauté pan, pushing the fish down into and amongst the leeks and apples. Cook gently for about 5 minutes, which will be sufficient time for the pieces of fish to cook through. Serve. This will keep warm – not simmering – for 10 minutes or so.

Mixed fish and shellfish chowder

This is a main course containing everything in one dish – the fish and shell-fish ratios can be made up of whatever you choose. If you want a dish for a family supper, leave out the shellfish and make up the quantity with fish, either smoked or unsmoked. I have made this with every type of fish and shellfish I can bring to mind, including smoked haddock, monkfish, cod, ling or whiting, and mussels, prawns, squid cut into rings, or scallops for a rather more special occasion. This has so much flavour, and at the same time it is an extremely nutritious main course, full of vegetables and fish – what could possibly be more delicious? And the saffron in the recipe elevates it to a more elegant overall taste.

A mandolin is helpful, to take the strain out of slicing the vegetables thinly. So much can be prepared in advance – the fish can all be felt and all bones removed and thrown away, and the fish cut into appropriate-sized chunks, then kept in a covered bowl in the fridge overnight. The vegetables can be prepared and the onions fried with the celery and fennel, to be reheated the following day if it is more convenient for you.

I don't think anything else is required to accompany this main course – it's all there, in the pot and then on the soup plate – you do need large soup plates to contain the liquid.

Serves 6

4 tbsps olive oil

2 onions, skinned and sliced very thinly

4 sticks of celery, washed, trimmed of stringy bits and sliced very thinly

2 rashers back bacon, fat cut off and the lean bacon sliced into thin strips

1–2 cloves of garlic, skinned and chopped

1 bulb of fennel, ends trimmed off and the fennel sliced as thinly as possible

2 carrots, peeled and sliced into fine matchsticks

6 medium-sized potatoes, peeled and sliced into matchsticks, as thin as possible

1.2 litres/2 pints fish or vegetable stock

2 generous pinches saffron strands

1kg/2lbs 4oz approx. fish and shellfish (ratio as you prefer)

4 tomatoes, skinned, quartered, seeded and sliced into thin strips

2 tbsps chopped parsley
lots of black pepper
salt to taste (you may well think it isn't necessary)

Feel the fish on a board and remove any bones you encounter. Cut the fish into chunks about 2cm/1 inch in size.

Heat the olive oil in a large saucepan or casserole and fry the onions, celery and bacon over a moderate heat for 7–10 minutes, stirring from time to time. Then add the garlic, fennel, carrots and potatoes, and cook for a further 2–3 minutes before pouring the stock into the saucepan. Stir in the saffron strands. Bring the liquid to a gentle simmer, half cover the pan with its lid and simmer gently until the carrot is quite soft when stuck with a fork. Add the prepared pieces of fish at this stage; they will take about 5 minutes to cook from when the liquid returns to simmering point – don't let it boil fast, because the pieces of vegetables will fall into bits.

Just before ladling into soup plates, add the sliced tomatoes, chopped parsley and pepper, tasting to see if any salt is required. Allow a minute for the tomatoes to heat through.

Main courses occasions

or special

THIS CHAPTER CONTAINS recipes that are a bit more special in their content, intended for those events when we all like to push out the boat and be slightly more extravagant. These times can be a family member returning home for a visit, birthdays, anniversaries, lunch or dinner parties – as far as I'm concerned, anything does as an excuse for a party! But we don't usually buy king scallops, for example, for an everyday supper dish; nor would we buy potted shrimps to turn into the delectable Shrimp Puff Pie (page 229) unless for a more special occasion. This chapter is full of ideas for just such a happening, but at the same time, many of the recipes are practical, and to a greater or lesser extent can be prepared in advance – vital to all of us who lead busy lives yet who love to eat as well and as deliciously as we can.

Cod baked with parsley and lemon pesto

This is such a favourite of mine. The pesto can be made two days in advance. The fish could be hake instead of cod; either can be prepared and coated with the pesto a day before cooking. I love this served with new potatoes mixed with mint, and with peas cooked with bacon and shallots. The pesto becomes quite sloppy around the fish as it bakes, so it provides its own sauce. The pesto itself is full of the flavours of parsley and lemon, but also a hint of chilli and far more than a hint of garlic.

Serves 6

6 pieces of filleted cod (or hake), each weighing about 175 g/6 oz

For the pesto **225 g/8 oz parsley**
25 g/1 oz coriander
2 fat cloves of garlic, skinned and chopped
½ tsp dried chilli flakes
½ tsp flaky salt, preferably Maldon
a good grinding of black pepper
300 ml/½ pint olive oil
finely grated rind of 2 lemons, well washed to remove preservative and dried before grating
2 tbsps lemon juice

Put the fish on a board, feel it carefully and remove any bones.

Make the pesto by putting the parsley and coriander into a food processor with the chopped garlic, chilli, salt and pepper. You will need to pack down the herbs. Whiz, gradually adding the olive oil in a thin steady trickle. Lastly, whiz in the lemon rinds and juice. Scrape the contents of the processor into a bowl, cover, and store it in the fridge. The olive oil will form a film on the surface after the pesto has been left for several hours, but don't worry: just stir it up to mix it in.

main courses for special occasions

Put the pieces of fish into an ovenproof dish. Spread the pesto over each piece of fish, dividing it evenly amongst them. If you are preparing the fish in advance, cover the dish with clingfilm before storing it in the fridge and be sure to allow it half an hour at room temperature before baking.

Bake in a moderate oven, 180°C/350°F/gas mark 4 (bottom-right oven in a four-door Aga), for 25–30 minutes. (Remember to remove the clingfilm before putting the dish into the oven!) Test by carefully forking apart the thickest part of a piece of fish to check that it parts into fat juicy flakes. If you think it looks rather undercooked, replace the dish in the oven for a further 5–10 minutes.

This dish will keep warm at a very low temperature for 20–30 minutes. It is also very good served cooled.

Spaghetti with crab, garlic, chilli, lemon and parsley

This recipe is both delicious to eat and very quick to assemble. It has often been a main course for a special occasion for our family here at Kinloch when I am pushed for time. Its success depends entirely on the quality of the crabmeat used. I have demonstrated up and down the country, using crabmeat kindly supplied by people local to where the demonstration has been, and sometimes the crab is bordering on the revolting. Such crabmeat is a world apart from ours, which, I have come to realize, is the best anywhere.

For this recipe, I use only the white crabmeat – I think this is the only recipe using crab where I do only use white, but the brown, softer crabmeat renders the pasta stodgy in texture and ruins the dish. A mixed-leaf salad, with a Dijon mustard vinaigrette, is all else required to complete this main course.

Serves 6

575 g/1¼ lb white crabmeat, of the finest quality
    that you can find
2 fat cloves of garlic, skinned and chopped very finely
1 red chilli (birdseye type for heat), seeds removed and the
    chilli chopped very finely (wear rubber gloves)
2 tbsps chopped parsley
300 ml/½ pint olive oil
finely grated rind of 2 lemons, washed well to remove
    preservative and dried before grating
1 tsp flaky salt, preferably Maldon
a good grinding of black pepper
675 g/1½ lb spaghetti

In a bowl, mix together the crabmeat, garlic, chilli, parsley and olive oil with the lemon rind and salt and pepper.

In a large saucepan of salted boiling water cook the spaghetti for about 5 minutes. Drain, then tip the drained spaghetti back into the saucepan and immediately mix in the contents of the crabmeat bowl. Mix very thoroughly. The olive oil will prevent the spaghetti strands sticking together, and the heat of the drained spaghetti will heat up the crabmeat. Serve.

Halibut coated in walnuts, and fried in butter with lemon

I would never have thought of using crushed walnuts as a coating for fish had I not eaten this on a wonderful summer holiday in the small coastal area of Basilicata, in Italy. The fish I ate that evening wasn't halibut but amberjack, a member of the grouper family, which we can't get here. Any firm-fleshed white fish will do for this – I suggest halibut, but you could just as well substitute cod, hake, whiting, ling or megrim.

Serves 6

6 pieces of filleted halibut, each weighing about 175 g/6 oz

For the coating **225 g/8 oz walnuts**
1 tsp salt, preferably Maldon
a good grinding of black pepper
1 tbsp chopped parsley
3 tbsps flour, sieved on to a plate
2 eggs, beaten with a fork, on a plate
50 g/2 oz butter and 3 tbsps olive oil

Put the walnuts into a sauté pan, and gently crush them with the end of a rolling pin. Over a moderate heat, dry-fry the nuts in the sauté pan for several minutes. This refreshes their taste and slightly toasts them. As stale walnuts tend to be bitter, it helps dispel the bitter taste. Add the salt and pepper to the dry-frying walnuts, then scoop the contents of the sauté pan on to a wide plate and leave to cool completely. Mix in the chopped parsley.

Dip each piece of fish first in the sieved flour, then in the beaten egg (I really do mean in this order) and, lastly, dip each side in the crushed nuts and parsley. Put the coated pieces of fish on to a baking tray lined with baking parchment. You can prepare the fish in the morning ready to cook that evening, but cover the 6 pieces of fish with another sheet of parchment, and keep the tray in the fridge.

main courses for special occasions

To cook, melt the butter and heat it together with the olive oil in a sauté pan and, when very hot, slip in the pieces of fish. When you put them into the sauté pan, leave them – don't be tempted to push them around with a fish slice. Left alone, they will cook and form a crisp, nutty crust and the fish will cook from within. After about 45–60 seconds, carefully turn each one over and leave to cook for the same length of time on the other side. If the butter and oil is hot enough, a golden crust should have formed. This is so quick to cook, but so good to eat. I like to serve it with leeks in a creamy lemon sauce, which doubles up as a vegetable and a sauce. But the Leek and Ginger Sauce (page 266) goes very well if you want an actual sauce. And I love courgettes, mandolin-sliced into spaghetti thickness, and stir-fried in olive oil with garlic, to go with it.

Halibut marinated in lime and chilli, with aromatic rice

This way of cooking fish for a special occasion is both convenient and delicious. The rice is an integral part of the whole, and the only accompaniment required would be a green vegetable – I would opt for courgettes, roasted in chunks in olive oil.

Serves 6

6 pieces of halibut, each weighing about 175 g /6 oz, skin and bones removed
300 ml/½ pint olive oil
2 cloves of garlic, skinned and chopped
finely grated rinds of 2 limes, well washed to remove
     preservative and dried before grating
2 tbsps strong soy sauce (e.g. Kikkoman's)
½ tsp dried chilli flakes
½ tsp salt
a good grinding of black pepper

For the rice   3 tbsps olive oil
3 large shallots, skinned and very finely sliced
2 cloves of garlic, skinned and chopped finely
5-cm/2-inch piece of fresh ginger, skin removed and the
     ginger finely chopped or coarsely grated
2 cardamom seeds, bashed
350 g /12 oz basmati rice
1.2 litres/2 pints chicken or vegetable stock, nearly boiling
½ tsp salt
a good grinding of black pepper
2 tbsps chopped parsley

main courses for special occasions

Start by marinating the halibut. In a bowl, mix together the olive oil, chopped garlic, lime rinds, soy sauce, chilli flakes, salt and pepper. Put the pieces of halibut into a wide, shallow, ovenproof dish and pour the marinade over them. Lift them up so that some marinade slips beneath them. Cover the dish with clingfilm, and leave it in the fridge overnight. Return it to room temperature for 30 minutes before baking.

To cook the rice, heat the olive oil in a large, preferably non-stick sauté pan or saucepan. Fry the thinly sliced shallots very well, until they are quite soft and transparent and beginning to turn golden at the edges. During their cooking time add the chopped garlic and ginger, stirring all in together well. Add the 2 bashed cardamom seeds and the rice. Stir and cook for 2–3 minutes. Then pour in the very hot stock, and don't stir again once the stock is added, but cover the pan with a folded tea towel and then its lid. Simmer gently for 5 minutes, then draw off the heat – don't lift the lid – and leave for 20–30 minutes. As it stands, the rice will absorb the liquid.

Meanwhile, cook the halibut. Cover a large baking tray or roasting tin with a sheet of baking parchment, lift the halibut from their marinade, scraping off any bits of garlic, and put the drained halibut on to the baking parchment. Cover with a second sheet of parchment, pressing it down on the fish. Bake in a moderate oven, 180°C/350°F/gas mark 4 (bottom-right oven in a four-door Aga), for 20–25 minutes; exactly how long depends on the thickness of the halibut, but test by carefully easing apart the middle of one of the pieces of fish to see if the juicy flakes of fish are cooked. If they look a bit undercooked for your liking, re-cover with the parchment and bake for a further 5 minutes.

Just before dishing up and serving, stir the salt and pepper and chopped parsley through the rice. If you can spot them, remove the cardamom seeds. Put a piece of halibut on each of six plates, and serve with the aromatic rice beside or underneath each piece of baked halibut.

Steam-baked halibut with julienne vegetables and saffron

This is an excellent main course for a special occasion when it is to be preceded and followed by rich courses. It is so very low in any fat content, and it has the added bonus of its vegetable accompaniment being part of the main dish. You can substitute any firm-fleshed white fish for the halibut suggested. The secret is to slice the vegetables as thinly as possible, which is really only achievable with a mandolin. Serve with new potatoes mixed with plenty of chopped mint.

Serves 6

2 medium-sized onions, skinned and very finely sliced
2 bulbs of fennel, trimmed and very thinly sliced
3 carrots, peeled and sliced into very thin matchsticks
3 medium-sized leeks, trimmed, cut into chunks about
    4 cm/2 inches, then sliced into very fine matchsticks
5-cm/2-inch piece of fresh root ginger, skin cut off and
    the ginger grated
1.2 litres/2 pints good vegetable or chicken stock
1 tsp saffron strands
juice and finely grated rind of 1 lime, well washed to remove
    preservative and dried before grating
½ tsp flaky salt, preferably Maldon
a good grinding of black pepper
6 pieces of filleted halibut, each weighing
    about 175 g/6 oz

Put all the prepared vegetables and grated ginger into a saucepan with the stock and the saffron and simmer gently for 10–15 minutes. Test to check that the vegetables are cooked by cutting into a stick of carrot, which is the vegetable which will need the longest cooking time. If it is still hard, continue to simmer the vegetables in the stock for a further 5 minutes. Strain off the cooking liquid, but keep it because it will make excellent soup. Mix the lime rind and juice into the cooked vegetables, with the salt and pepper.

Lay a sheet of baking parchment on a baking tray. Put the pieces of halibut on this, and top each with an equal portion of cooked vegetables. Cover the whole with a second sheet of baking parchment and bake in a moderate heat, 180°C/350°F/gas mark 4 (bottom-right oven in a four-door Aga), for 20–25 minutes; give it a bit longer if the fish is much thicker than 4 cm/1½ inches.

Serve by simply lifting the pieces of fish with their vegetable coverings on to each of six warmed plates.

Roast streaky bacon-wrapped monkfish, with peas and mint

The bacon for this – indeed for any eating whatsoever – must be the finest. This means dry-cured, and very thinly sliced. The bacon imparts its flavour to the monkfish, and bacon and fish and shellfish have a terrific taste affinity. The fat in the streaky bacon acts as a protective barrier to prevent the fish drying out as it roasts. The pea and mint sauce, on which the sliced roast monkfish is served, both looks good and tastes delicious with the bacon and fish. A good ratatouille is excellent with this, as are new potatoes in season.

Serves 6

1.2 kg/2½ lb monkfish fillets, all membrane trimmed off
    (easy, with a really sharp knife)
approx. 18 rashers of streaky bacon, smoked or
    unsmoked (I prefer to use smoked)
2 tbsps olive oil

For the pea and   **2 tbsps olive oil**
mint sauce   **2 shallots, each skinned and chopped**
450 g/1 lb fresh young peas, weighed when shelled
    (if unavailable, use frozen petits pois)
300 ml/½ pint chicken or vegetable stock
about 1 tbsp mint, preferably applemint, leaves
    stripped from their stalks
300 ml/½ pint double cream
½ tsp salt
a good grinding of black pepper
a grating of nutmeg

Make the sauce first. Heat the olive oil in a saucepan and fry the chopped shallots for 3–4 minutes, until they are quite soft and transparent. Then add the peas and stock; half cover the pan with a lid, and simmer very gently for 2 minutes. Take the pan off the heat, cool

main courses for special occasions

a bit before liquidizing the contents of the saucepan with the mint to a smooth purée – you may need to sieve this to get the required velvety texture; it will depend on how sharp the blades are in your blender or Magimix. Rinse out the saucepan and put the purée back in it, stir in the double cream, taste, then season with salt, pepper and nutmeg. Reheat, gently simmering the sauce.

Wrap each monkfish fillet in streaky bacon. Line a roasting tin with baking parchment – to make washing up easier afterwards – and put the bacon-wrapped monkfish on this. Brush each with olive oil, and roast in a hot oven, 220°C/450°F/gas mark 7 (roasting oven in an Aga), for 15–20 minutes; exactly how long depends on the thickness of the monkfish fillets. Take the roasting tin out of the oven, leave for 5 minutes before lifting the fillets on to a board, and, with a sharp knife, slice them diagonally, in slices about 2.5 cm/1 inch thick.

Spoon some of the pea and mint puréed sauce on to each of six warmed plates and divide the slices of roast monkfish between them. Alternatively, put the sauce over the base of a large serving dish, and arrange the sliced monkfish on top.

Monkfish, stir-fried with red peppers, lemongrass, ginger and garlic

This is a most delicious combination of flavours, and it is highly nutritious as well as tasting absolutely delicious. All that is required to go with it is boiled basmati rice and a mixed-leaf salad. The main course itself needs no garnish – the red pepper strips are colour enough. And the monkfish is the perfect fish for this recipe because it holds its shape during stir-frying – cod, or hake, for example, falls into flat juicy flakes if the fish is as fresh as it should be.

Serves 6

900 g/2 lb monkfish fillets, trimmed of all membrane and
    cut into 2.5-cm/1-inch chunks
1 stick of lemongrass, sliced finely
12 spring onions, trimmed, and diagonally sliced into pieces
    about 2.5 cm/1 inch
5-cm/2-inch piece of root ginger, skin pared off
    and the ginger coarsely grated or chopped finely
4 fat cloves of garlic, skinned and chopped finely
1 rounded tsp cornflour
4 tbsps medium sherry
3 tbsps strong soy sauce
3 tsps sesame oil
4 tbsps olive oil
3 red peppers, cut in half, seeds scooped away, and
    sliced as thinly as possible
300 ml/½ pint chicken or vegetable stock
2 tbsps chopped coriander

Put the pieces of monkfish into a bowl, cover with clingfilm and leave the bowl in the fridge till you are ready to cook. Mix together the lemongrass, spring onions, ginger and garlic in a bowl and cover with clingfilm. Mix together the cornflour, sherry, soy sauce and sesame oil in a jug or bowl.

When you are ready to cook, heat the olive oil in a large casserole or sauté pan and stir-fry the sliced red peppers over a high heat until they are soft – about 3–4 minutes. Then, still with the heat high under the pan, add the spring onions, garlic, ginger and lemongrass and cook, stirring, till they soften – a further 2–3 minutes. Then stir in the contents of the cornflour and sherry mixture, stirring up the cornflour well from the bottom of the jug or bowl, because it will have sunk to the base of the container. Stir continuously as the mixture thickens and bubbles, and stir in the stock, stirring till it returns to simmering. Then put the pieces of monkfish into the pan and mix them in well. Cook for 2–3 minutes. The pieces of fish will turn opaque. Just before serving stir in the chopped coriander.

Chargrilled monkfish with shellfish, chilli and lime, in crème fraîche and lime dressing

This is one of our most favourite of all special occasion main courses. I unashamedly repeat it here because it must be in a book on fish cooking. It was made up – composed, if you like – for the huge family dinner the evening before our second daughter's, Isabella's, wedding to Tom in 2000. For me it is always associated with that happy weekend. At that time, none of us had an inkling that they would move up, as they did two years later, to live and work with us here at Kinloch. So, did we but know it, their marriage also heralded a living and working partnership between us and them that I give thanks for daily!

You can use any shellfish combination. But I do recommend chargrilling the monkfish – even if it means lighting a barbecue in the depths of winter it is worth it for the taste. If you like you can alter the ratio of the fish and shellfish, but end up with 1.2 kg/2½ lb in total.

Serves 6

900 g/2 lb monkfish fillets, trimmed of all membrane
225 g/8 oz cooked shellfish (crabmeat and langoustines, for example)

For the marinade 4 tbsps olive oil
juice and finely grated rind of 2 limes, well washed to remove
    preservative and dried before grating
½ small red onion, skinned and very finely diced
1 red chilli, slit open, seeds removed, and the chilli
    chopped finely (wear rubber gloves)
½ tsp salt
½ tsp caster sugar
a good grinding of black pepper
2 tbsps chopped coriander

main courses for special occasions

300 ml/½ pint crème fraîche   *For the dressing*
finely grated rind of 1 lime, washed well as above
1 tbsp chopped coriander
½ tsp salt
a good grinding of black pepper

In a bowl, mix together all the marinade ingredients.

Brush each monkfish fillet with olive oil before chargrilling. Cook the fillets for 1–2 minutes, depending on their thickness, turning them over so that they cook evenly. As they cook, remove them from the chargrill and put them on a board. Slice them into chunks about 2.5 cm/1 inch in size. Put them into a large bowl with the shellfish, and mix the marinade into the fish and shellfish thoroughly. Cover the bowl with clingfilm and leave it in the fridge (or a cool larder, if the weather is cold) for several hours, or overnight (then in the fridge).

Mix together the ingredients for the dressing. Mix the dressing into the contents of the bowl to serve, or, if you prefer, serve the dressing separately.

Monkfish with tomatoes, garlic and black olives

Monkfish is a most useful fish because it keeps its shape while it cooks, unlike cod, for example, which readily falls into flakes. This dish can be just as delicious eaten cold, on warm summer evenings, in which case drizzle a bit more olive oil over the fish, tomatoes and olives before serving.

Serves 6

900 g/2 lb trimmed monkfish tails
3 tbsps good olive oil
2 medium onions, skinned and sliced finely
1 large garlic clove, skinned and chopped finely
½ tsp dried chilli flakes
8 tomatoes, skinned, sliced in wedges and seeds thrown away
8–12 good black olives, stoned and chopped
a pinch of sugar
a pinch of salt
freshly ground black pepper
1 tbsp chopped fresh basil

If the monkfish isn't trimmed of its membrane, do this using a really sharp knife. Cut each monkfish tail into chunks about 2.5 cm/1 inch. Heat the olive oil and sauté the sliced onions over a moderate heat till they are really soft – about 5–7 minutes – stirring from time to time to prevent them from turning too golden brown. Add the garlic and the chilli, cook for a minute, then add the fish. Stir till the fish turns opaque, then add the tomatoes. Cook for a further couple of minutes and stir in the olives, sugar, salt and pepper. Just before serving stir in the chopped basil. If you are making this in the winter months, you can substitute pesto for fresh basil, using a good teaspoonful. This is good served with either new potatoes, boiled basmati rice, or with spaghetti, tossed when cooked in olive oil, with chopped parsley and with more finely chopped garlic, too, if you like – I do!

main courses for special occasions

Monkfish medallions with grapes and almonds

I like to use red, seedless grapes for this, just cut in half. The fried shallots and lemon juice, together with the toasted flaked almonds, give a really delicious and slightly different accompaniment to the marinated monkfish. It looks good, too! Serve with a purée of roast root vegetables, and green beans or sugarsnap peas.

Serves 6

300 ml/½ pint olive oil   *For the marinade*
a good grinding of black pepper
2 tbsps chopped parsley

1.2 kg/2½ lb trimmed monkfish fillets, sliced thickly
to give 18 slices (3 per person)

4 tbsps olive oil   *For the grape*
4 large shallots, each skinned and diced very finely   *mixture*
75 g/3 oz flaked almonds
½ tsp salt
a good grinding of black pepper
finely grated rind of 2 lemons, well washed to remove
preservative and dried before grating
675 g/1½ lb seedless red or black grapes, washed
and cut in half
2 tbsps chopped parsley

Mix together the marinade ingredients. Put the sliced monkfish into a wide dish, and spoon the marinade over the fish. Cover the dish with clingfilm, and leave overnight, in the larder if you have one, or the fridge. Remember to return the dish to room temperature for 30 minutes before cooking the fish.

For the grape mixture, heat the 4 tablespoons of olive oil in a sauté

Monkfish medallions with grapes and almonds

pan and fry the finely diced shallots for several minutes, until very soft and transparent. Then add the almonds, salt, pepper and lemon rinds, and fry, stirring occasionally to prevent burning, until the almonds are toasted-looking. Then add the halved grapes, and cook for several minutes, stirring occasionally, until the grapes soften. Lastly, stir in the chopped parsley. Keep this mixture warm until you are ready to serve it – it won't need to be very hot from the pan, just warm, so it can easily be made a couple of hours in advance.

To cook the slices of monkfish, heat a large sauté pan until very hot. Lift the slices of fish from the olive oil marinade (but leave on any chopped parsley: it will be delicious when seared and crispy), pat dry and sear them in the very hot, dry sauté pan. Sear for 40–45 seconds on each side, then lift them on to a large, warmed serving plate.

To serve, put a spoonful of grape, shallot and almond mixture into the centre of each piece of seared monkfish.

Chargrilled monkfish with braised lettuce, peas and spring onions

The monkfish is wrapped in very thinly sliced streaky bacon for this dish, which prevents the fish becoming dried out during its chargrilling, itself a very drying form of cooking. I love the taste of chargrilled foods, and, outside summer months, owning a Cobb barbecue has meant that I can chargrill in my kitchen. These Cobbs were invented to be used in the galleys of boats, so in a kitchen they are fine, and mean that we can chargrill year round without an outside barbecue.

The braised lettuce with peas and spring onions is a delicious foil for the fish and bacon, and at the same time doubles up as a vegetable. But I suggest very well-mashed potatoes, with horseradish and chopped chives beaten into the potatoes, as an accompaniment. If you are wondering whether the overall flavour of the chargrilled monkfish with the braised lettuce, peas and spring onions might be slightly bland, have no fear: the lemon in the ingredients is the answer!

Serves 6

1.2 kg/2½ lb trimmed monkfish fillets, all membrane removed
18 rashers of thinly sliced streaky bacon, smoked or unsmoked
olive oil

3 tbsps olive oil *For the braised*
12 spring onions, trimmed, ends cut off, and sliced lengthways *vegetables*
1–2 fat cloves of garlic, skinned and chopped finely
450 g/1 lb shelled peas, *or* frozen petits pois
6 firm lettuces (e.g. Cobb), trimmed of any outer leaves and quartered
1 tbsp strong soya sauce (kecap manis, or Kikkoman's)
juice and finely grated rind of 1 lemon, washed well to remove
preservative and dried before grating
300 ml/½ pint chicken or vegetable stock
lots of black pepper (no need for salt:
the soy sauce contributes enough

Chargrilled monkfish with braised lettuce, peas and spring onions

Prepare the fish by wrapping each fillet in streaky bacon once you have trimmed all membrane off. Brush each bacon-wrapped fillet with olive oil, and leave, covered, in the fridge for several hours if it is more convenient for you to prepare the fish well in advance. But be sure that the fish has half an hour at room temperature before chargrilling.

To braise the vegetables, heat the 3 tablespoons of olive oil in a large sauté pan and add the sliced spring onions. Stir-fry for a couple of minutes, then add the chopped garlic and cook for a further half minute before adding the peas and the lettuce quarters to the contents of the sauté pan. Mix the soy sauce, grated lemon rind and juice and stock together, and season this with black pepper, then pour it over the contents of the saucepan. Cover the pan with its lid, and simmer the contents gently over a moderate heat for 10–15 minutes.

When the coals are white hot, put the bacon-wrapped fish on to the grill and cook for 1–2 minutes (how long depends on the thickness of the fish, it varies so much) before turning it over to grill on the other side. When the bacon is cooked, remove the fish and bacon from the grill on to a board. Slice in thick – about 4-cm/1½-inch – diagonal slices and serve alongside a spoonful of the braised vegetables.

main courses for special occasions

Prawns with slightly devilled sauce

This is a sumptuous main course for a special occasion. It is very easy to make, and the sauce actually benefits from being made hours in advance, because the flavours settle down together as it sits. It isn't very hot and spicy – hence the 'slightly devilled' in the title. Use the best prawns you can buy – for us, this means succulent langoustines, but there are a number of good prawn alternatives.

I like to heap boiled basmati rice around the prawns in their sauce, but first I mix the rice with olive oil and herbs, which makes it look much more attractive as well as taste far more interesting – a perfect foil for the creamy prawns.

Serves 6

600 ml/1 pint creamy crème fraîche
1 small red onion, skinned and diced finely and neatly
2 tbsps Worcester sauce
1 tsp Tabasco
2 tbsps lemon juice
2 tbsps chopped parsley and snipped chives, mixed
½ tsp salt
a good grinding of black pepper
900 g/2 lb shelled prawns – cut them in half if they are very large

Tip the crème fraîche into a mixing bowl and add the finely diced red onion, the Worcester sauce, Tabasco, lemon juice, herbs and salt and pepper. Mix together thoroughly. Then mix in the prawns. Heap the contents of the bowl on to a serving plate – no need for garnishing; the herbs perk up the appearance as well as contributing their flavours. Surround with rice, if you like, as mentioned in the introduction to the recipe, or with assorted salad leaves.

Hot-smoked salmon kedgeree with quails' eggs and saffron

Kedgeree can be a disgusting dish, or it can be food for the gods. It is a great favourite in our family because it is rice-based and we all love rice; the long-grain rice that I use for this (and for all things not requiring short-grain or risotto-type rice) is basmati. Smoked fish is essential to a good kedgeree – a white fish kedgeree is pretty dreary eating. I fry a small amount of medium-strength curry powder in with the finely diced onions as the basis for my recipe, and I use the milk and water the fish cooked in for cooking the rice – that way, I get twice the flavour from the smoked fish.

Some people put raisins or sultanas in their kedgeree; I like this, but no other member of our family does so I tend not to include them. Chopped parsley stirred through the kedgeree just before serving really makes a great difference, not only to the overall appearance of the dish but also to the taste. I also like to add chopped hardboiled eggs, but eggs do not freeze well so I leave them out if I am going to freeze the kedgeree. (You can freeze kedgeree in a well-buttered ovenproof dish; dot the surface with bits of butter before freezing and defrost overnight in the fridge; bake in a moderate oven – 180°C/350°F/gas mark 4, bottom-right oven in a four-door Aga – for 35–40 minutes, forking through the contents to distribute the melting bits of butter. The dish must have a lid to prevent the surface rice drying out.)

Serves 6

1 fillet of smoked haddock
1 onion, skinned and cut in half
1.5 litres/2½ pints milk and water mixed – ratio half and half

For the kedgeree   25 g/1 oz butter and 2 tbsps olive oil
4 banana shallots, with violet-tinted flesh, skinned and
    finely chopped, *or* 8 smaller shallots
375 g/12 oz long-grain rice (I use basmati)
2 good pinches of saffron strands
675 g/1½ lb hot-smoked salmon, flaked, skin removed
2–3 tbsps chopped parsley, preferably flat-leaved
12 quails' eggs, hardboiled, shelled and cut in half
lots of freshly ground black pepper
75 g/3 oz butter, cut in bits

main courses for special occasions

Put the smoked haddock, onion, milk and water into a saucepan over a moderate heat, and bring the liquid to simmering point. Take the pan off the heat and leave to cool completely. Strain the fish and reserve the stock in a jug.

In a large sauté pan, or saucepan which has a lid, melt the butter and heat it together with the oil. Sauté the chopped shallots until they are very soft and transparent. Stir in the rice, and stir for 2–3 minutes, so that each grain of rice is coated in buttery oil and is very well mixed with the shallots. Add the saffron. Pour in the strained smoked haddock stock till it comes to about 2.5 cm/1 inch above the level of the rice in the pan; when you add the liquid initially there will be a whoosh of steam – wait till this subsides to see the depth of liquid above the rice. Don't stir again once the liquid has been added to the pan. Replace the pan on the heat, cover with a tea towel and the lid, and cook on a gentle heat for 5 minutes. Then take the pan off the heat and leave for 15 minutes (still covered). By this time the liquid should have been absorbed by the rice, and the rice should be cooked.

With a fork, so as not to break up the flakes of fish, add the hot-smoked salmon, the chopped parsley and the halved quails' eggs to the pan. Season with pepper, and at this point add the bits of butter. Fork everything together over a gentle heat, and when you are satisfied that the heat from the rice and the gentle heat on which the pan is sitting have heated through the salmon and eggs, serve.

Baked fillet of organic salmon with carrot, shallot and ginger timbales

This is so convenient, and it tastes delicious. It is a perfect main course for a special occasion. The timbale mixture can be made a day in advance, but remember to give it a good stir before you divide the mixture between the oiled ramekins or moulds. When baked, the timbales have to stand for 10–15 minutes before being turned out on to warmed plates or on to a large serving plate, and they come to no harm if they stand for much longer, kept warm in a gentle heat. So not only do they taste very good but this is a main course of extreme convenience. Serve it with almost any of the hot sauces from pages 261–73); my own favourites are Sauce Bercy, or Shallot, White Wine and Saffron Cream Sauce. You could possibly accompany it with sautéed potatoes, and either a mixed-leaf salad or mangetouts, both potatoes and mangetouts giving a good contrasting texture to the salmon and the soft texture of the timbales.

Serves 6

6 pieces of filleted, organically farmed salmon
   (or wild salmon, in season)
175 g/6 oz butter, cut into 6 bits

For the timbales 4 tbsps olive oil
4 large torpedo or banana shallots, with violet-tinged flesh,
   or 2 small onions, skinned and chopped
900 g/2 lb carrots, weighed before peeling, peeled and cut into chunks
5-cm/approx. 2-inch piece of fresh root ginger, skin cut off and the ginger chopped
600 ml/1 pint vegetable or chicken stock
300 ml/½ pint double cream
3 large eggs
1 teaspoon flaky salt, preferably Maldon
a good grinding of black pepper
a grating of nutmeg
2 tbsps chives, finely snipped with scissors
   (optional, for garnish)

main courses for special occasions

Put the salmon on a board and feel it carefully, removing any bones you encounter.

Heat the olive oil in a sauté pan or large saucepan, add the chopped shallots or onions, and fry, stirring occasionally, until they are quite soft and turning golden at the edges – about 5 minutes over a moderate heat. Add the chopped carrots and ginger to the pan, and cook for a further 5 minutes, stirring to prevent any danger of the mixture scorching. Add the stock, cover the pan with its lid and cook over a moderate heat – not fast – for 10–15 minutes, or until when you stick a knife into a bit of carrot it feels quite soft. Cool. Strain off the liquid – there won't be much – and put the contents of the pan into a food processor. Whiz till smooth, then whiz in the cream and the eggs, one by one. Season with salt, pepper and nutmeg, and pour and scrape this mixture into a measure jug.

Rub six ramekins or moulds with olive oil. Divide the carrot mixture evenly between the oiled ramekins, put them into a roasting tin and pour boiling water into the tin, to come halfway up the sides of the ramekins. Bake in a moderate oven, 180°C/350°F/gas mark 4 (bottom-right oven in a four-door Aga), for 30–35 minutes, or until the tops of each feel quite firm. Take them out of the oven, and leave them to stand in the roasting tin and water for 10–15 minutes.

To cook the salmon, lay a sheet of baking parchment on a baking tray. Put the pieces of salmon on to this, put a piece of butter on each and cover with a second sheet of baking parchment. Bake in a moderate heat, 180°C/350°F/gas mark 4 (bottom-right oven in a four-door Aga), for 15–20 minutes, or until when you gently prise apart the thickest part of a piece of cooked salmon with two forks, the fish flakes. If it is thick and not cooked, re-cover the fish and cook for a further 5 minutes or so.

Turn the timbales out by running the blade of a knife around the inside of each ramekin or mould, and shake them gently on to the warmed plates. Put a piece of steam-baked salmon beside each and, if you like, scatter very finely snipped chives over each piece of fish and timbale.

Coulibiac of salmon

This is my version of the classic, omitting the mushrooms and rice correctly found in a coulibiac. I much prefer my version, immodest though that sounds, but I don't see the need for rice with puffed pastry. This is so convenient, because it can be made a day ahead of baking, providing that you brush the puff pastry with beaten egg and then cover with clingfilm before storing the baking tray in the fridge. Take it into room temperature for half an hour before baking it. With the suggested sauce as accompaniment – which can also be made a day in advance, then reheated before serving – this is such an elegant main course. I made it for the lunch following the christening of our first grandson, Billy, and so I put into practice what I preach! Accompany it with a green vegetable – my old favourite, sugarsnap peas, stir-fried with garlic, ginger and soya sauce, and a salad, either mixed-leaf or tomato. And new potatoes, if you like, but I don't think they are necessary.

Any leftover salmon is very good eaten cold with mayonnaise.

Serves 6

900 g/2 lb filleted organically farmed salmon
50 g/2 oz butter
4 banana shallots, with violet-tinted flesh, skinned and finely sliced
½ cucumber, peeled, cut lengthways in half, seeded and
    diced thumbnail-size
½ tsp salt
a good grinding of black pepper
675 g/1½ lb puff pastry (I use Bell's or Saxby's)
1 egg, beaten

For the sauce 3 shallots, skinned and very finely sliced
300 ml/½ pint dry white wine
finely grated rind of 1 lemon, washed well to remove
    preservative and dried before grating
300 ml/½ pint double cream
½ tsp salt
a good grinding of black pepper

To prepare the salmon, lay it on a board, feel it carefully and remove all bones and skin.

Melt the butter in a wide saucepan or sauté pan, and sauté the diced shallots and the diced cucumber together for several minutes, until the shallots are very soft. Season with salt and pepper. Cool.

Roll out two-thirds of the pastry so that it is bigger than the filleted piece of fish by a margin of about 4 cm/1½ inches. Put the (skinned) filleted salmon on this. Spoon over the cooled shallot and cucumber mixture. Roll out the remaining pastry to an oblong to cover the salmon, and put this over the salmon. Brush around the edges with beaten egg, and crimp the edges firmly together. Put the salmon en croûte on to a baking tray lined with baking parchment. Slash in four or five places down the top of the pastry, and garnish, if you like, with pastry fish. Brush the whole thing with the rest of the beaten egg. Cover with clingfilm and put in a cool place, a larder or fridge, until you bake it, in a fairly hot oven, 200°C/400°F/gas mark 6 (roasting oven in an Aga), for 30–35 minutes, or till well puffed up and deeply golden brown.

For the sauce, put the diced shallots into a saucepan with the white wine. Over a moderate heat, simmer the wine till it has almost reduced away. Then add the lemon rind and cream, salt and pepper, and simmer, stirring, until it is as thick as you would like – about 2 minutes' simmering is usually enough.

Baked salmon John Tovey, with lemon and butter fried cucumber

John Tovey was such a great influence in my life during the 1980s. He was such a character, and wickedly funny – still is, I hope, but not, alas, in the UK any longer; I think he is now living in South Africa. He taught me to cook salmon like this, and it is the simplest and best method.

We often serve salmon with this butter and lemon fried cucumber accompaniment for the Kinloch guests. Hot cucumber is delicious as a vegetable accompaniment, but it also provides a slight contrasting texture to the fish. I use clarified butter for this, not olive oil. Clarifying butter is the easiest thing to do – see the recipe – and makes all the difference to the taste. New potatoes are the perfect starch accompaniment, and nothing beats hollandaise sauce (pages 261–2) with all of these ingredients.

Serves 6

6 pieces of filleted salmon, skin removed, each weighing
    about 175 g/6 oz
6 pieces of butter, each weighing 25 g/1 oz

For the clarified butter   110 g/8 oz butter

For the cucumber   110 g/4 oz clarified butter
2 large banana or torpedo shallots, with violet-tinged flesh,
    skinned and sliced very thinly
3 cucumbers, peeled, cut in chunks each about 6 cm/2½ inches,
    each chunk halved, seeded and cut into 4–5 sticks
1 tbsp chopped dill
finely grated rind of 1 lemon, well washed to remove
    preservative and dried before grating
½ tsp salt
a good grinding of black pepper

To clarify the butter, put the butter in a saucepan in a warm place – **not** on direct heat, however low – and allow the butter to melt very, very slowly over an hour, if necessary. As it melts so slowly, the milky part sinks to the bottom of the pan and the clarified butter sits on top. Carefully – so as not to allow any curdy bits – pour the clarified butter into a bowl. Throw away the contents of the saucepan which remain on the bottom of the pan as you wash it up. You will use only half the clarified butter you have made for this recipe, but keep the rest in a covered bowl in the fridge to use later.

Put the pieces of salmon on a non-stick baking tray. Put a piece of butter on each piece of fish. Don't season the fish. Bake in a very hot oven, 220°C/450°F/gas mark 7 (roasting oven in an Aga), for 5 minutes. The fish should then be perfectly cooked.

For the cucumber, heat 110 g/4 oz of the clarified butter in a large sauté pan and fry the sliced shallots in this for several minutes, until they are completely transparent. Then add the prepared cucumber, the dill, grated lemon rind, salt and pepper. Cook over a moderately high heat, stirring but not continuously, for 7–10 minutes.

Serve, with the cucumber handed separately, or spooned beside each piece of fish, on warmed plates.

Salmon, tomato and basil filo parcels

These are delicious, with the contrast of crisp, crunchy pastry and soft fish. And the flavour is so good with the combined tomatoes, basil and salmon. I think that the tomato and basil mixture is better with salmon than with any other type of fish. This is a filling main course, so beware too heavy a first course or pud on either side of it. And I think that potatoes are superfluous. I recommend roasted carrots and shallots with grated lemon rind, and, possibly, sugarsnap peas, stir-fried with a small amount of ginger and garlic and a dash of soy sauce.

Serves 6

6 pieces of filleted salmon, skin and bones removed,
    each weighing 150–175 g/5–6 oz
6 sheets of filo pastry
175 g/6 oz butter, melted

For the tomato and basil mixture
6 ripe tomatoes, skinned, halved, seeds removed,
    and the flesh chopped
1 handful of basil leaves
finely grated rind of 1 lemon, washed well to remove
    preservative and dried before grating
½ tsp salt
lots of black pepper
2 tbsps olive oil

Mix together well all the ingredients for the tomato and basil mixture. The resulting mixture should be almost a mush, but don't be tempted to pulverize the ingredients in a food processor – it just doesn't work.

Lay a sheet of filo on a work surface and brush it entirely with melted butter. Cover with a second sheet of filo pastry and brush this, too, with melted butter. Cut the double filo in half widthways.

Lay a piece of salmon on each half, in the middle. Put a spoonful of the tomato mixture on top of each piece of salmon and fold the filo over to make a parcel. Brush entirely with melted butter. Repeat this until all the salmon and filo is made up into 6 filo parcels. Put these on to a non-stick baking tray, and bake in a hot oven, 220°C/420°F/gas mark 7 (roasting oven in an Aga), for 15 minutes. Serve as soon as possible.

These parcels are best assembled not too long before being cooked, but you can make the tomato and basil mixture in advance by one day, which does help to get ahead!

Scallops with squid, lemon and parsley

This is a very simple dish, but an excellent example of how, if you buy the very best produce, you need do so little with it. For those who, like us, love shellfish, this is a perfect main course, fitting for a special occasion. But it is essential that the squid is prepared with care, and that neither the squid nor the scallops are overcooked. With this, I think that a good salad, perhaps young spinach leaves, avocado and crispy bits of bacon, is an excellent accompaniment.

Serves 6

450 g/1 lb squid
18 king scallops
4 tbsps olive oil
2 fat cloves of garlic, chopped finely
juice of ½ lemon
½ tsp salt
2 tbsps chopped parsley, flat or curly leaved

First check that the squid has been cleaned thoroughly. Look for a plastic-like end and pull firmly – this is the end of the quill, and the innards should emerge with it as you pull it out. Under running cold water, rinse out the interior of the squid, dry as best you can with kitchen paper, and slice it into rings, chopping the tentacles. Soak the prepared squid in milk for several hours, then drain off the milk and pat the squid dry on kitchen paper.

Take the scallops and remove the small strip of white muscle that connects the shellfish to its shell (use scissors).

main courses for special occasions

Heat the olive oil in a sauté pan and, over a high heat, fry the pieces of squid, stirring them around in the sauté pan and cooking for 1–2 minutes. Scoop the fried squid on to a warmed dish.

Keep the heat high and sear the scallops for barely 30 seconds on each side. Remove them to the warm dish and lower the heat in the pan. Add the garlic and lemon juice and stir-fry, with the salt and chopped parsley, for a minute, then mix this in amongst the cooked squid and scallops.

Serve, three scallops per warmed plate with a small heap of squid in the centre.

Seared scallops with Jerusalem artichoke risotto

This is such a dream team of taste combinations. I am so often asked what would be my favourite dish – an impossible question to answer because there are so very many favourites for different times of the year and for different occasions, but if I was pressed for a response, I am pretty sure that Scallops with Artichoke Risotto would be my answer. It is hard to fathom just why the flavours of scallops and artichokes are so mutually delectable, but believe me, they are. All that's needed to accompany this main course would be either a mixed-leaf salad, or a green vegetable such as sugarsnap peas.

If the main course has had no preceding first course, then you might possibly allow 4 scallops per person, but judge the appetites for yourself – you will know your guests, and age has a great deal to do with capacity. Scallops are filling, and so is risotto, therefore I think that 3 large, king scallops are a perfect amount.

Serves 6

18 king scallops, corals left on
4 tbsps olive oil
a good grinding of black pepper

For the risotto 900 g/2 lb Jerusalem artichokes, weighed before peeling
1.5 litres/3 pints chicken or vegetable stock
6 tbsps olive oil
2 onions, *or* 4 banana or torpedo shallots with
   violet-tinged flesh, skinned and diced finely
450 g/1 lb risotto rice, either arborio or carnaroli
150 ml/¼ pint dry white wine
50 g/2 oz butter, cut into 4 bits
1 tsp flaky salt, preferably Maldon
a good grinding of black pepper
2 tbsps chopped parsley

Peel the artichokes and cut them into fairly even-sized bits. Put them into a saucepan with the stock, and let the stock simmer and the artichokes cook for about 10–15 minutes. Stick a fork into an artichoke piece and test if it is soft. Cool, then liquidize the contents of the saucepan and keep the liquid for the risotto.

Cut with scissors – the easiest way – the small ridge of white from the edge of each scallop. (This is the bit which sticks the scallop to the shell and is tough and chewy to eat if left in place.) Put the scallops into a dish and cover with the 4 tablespoons of olive oil and a good grinding of black pepper. Leave for a couple of hours and, if you remember, turn the scallops once during this time.

To make the risotto, heat the olive oil in a sauté pan, and fry the diced onions or shallots for several minutes, until they are quite soft and transparent looking. Then stir in the rice, and cook, stirring, for about 1 minute. The aim is to coat each grain of rice with oil. Add the white wine, and stir until the wine evaporates, which will take less than a minute. Then add some of the artichoke stock, and cook gently, stirring occasionally, until the rice has absorbed the liquid. Add more artichoke stock, and let this too be absorbed by the rice. Continue until all the liquid has been added and absorbed, but don't let the risotto become stodgy. Then stir in the pieces of butter, season with salt and pepper, and, just before serving, add the chopped parsley.

To cook the scallops, heat a large sauté pan until it is very hot, then sear the scallops in the hot, dry pan for about 30 seconds on each side.

Serve the risotto in a small mound in the centre of each of six warmed plates, with three seared scallops at the edge. Eat as soon as possible.

King scallops mornay with mushroom duxelles

I consider king scallops to be one of life's most luxurious of all luxury foods. I love them seared, but I love them too in this recipe, where the scallops are seared briefly over a very high heat, then put on a bed of mushroom duxelles, with a thin layer of the best béchamel sauce, grated cheese to cover the sauce, then grilled. This is a heavenly dish, and best eaten with plain boiled basmati rice, and with nutmeg and butter spinach.

Serves 6

18 king scallops, the small ridge of tough white muscle
   snipped off with scissors
6 tbsps olive oil
a good grinding of black pepper

For the mushroom duxelles
3 tbsps olive oil and 50 g/2 oz butter
2 shallots, skinned and very finely diced
900 g/2 lb mushrooms, wiped and chopped very finely,
   until they are almost minced
1 level tsp salt
a good grinding of black pepper
a grating of nutmeg

For the béchamel sauce
50 g/2 oz butter
1 rounded tbsp flour
750 ml/1¼ pints milk
½ tsp salt
a good grinding of black pepper
a grating of nutmeg

75 g/3 oz grated cheese (I use Isle of Mull Cheddar)
2 tbsps snipped chives and chopped parsley, mixed

main courses for special occasions

Put the scallops into a wide dish and spoon 6 tablespoons of olive oil over them. Grind black pepper liberally all over, cover the dish, and leave for several hours.

Melt the butter and heat it together with the olive oil in a sauté pan. Fry the finely diced shallots for 3–5 minutes, stirring, until they are soft. Turn up the heat under the pan, and add the almost minced mushrooms – there will look to be quite a lot, but the amount decreases as they cook. Stir and fry the contents of the sauté pan until the mushrooms are cooked down in quantity. Season with salt, pepper and nutmeg. Spread this mixture over the base of an ovenproof dish, sufficiently large to hold the seared scallops in a single layer.

Cook the scallops by heating a wide, shallow sauté pan until it is very, very hot indeed, but put no oil at all into the pan. Lift the scallops from their dish and put them into the very hot pan for 20 seconds on each side. Lift them on to the prepared mushroom mixture in the ovenproof dish.

Make the sauce by melting the butter in a saucepan and stirring in the tablespoon of flour. Let this cook for a minute, then, stirring continuously, gradually add the milk, until it is all included and the sauce boils. Season with salt, pepper and nutmeg. Pour the sauce over the scallops. Mix the grated cheese with the chopped herbs and scatter evenly over the entire surface of the scallops, then put the dish under a pre-heated grill, just until the cheese melts.

There are several do-ahead aspects to this recipe, although it is best if the whole thing is assembled and grilled in one go, immediately before serving. But you can make the mushroom duxelles a day in advance, provided you reheat it before spreading it over the base of the ovenproof dish.

You can also make the sauce a day in advance, but once you draw the pan off the heat, immediately cover the surface of the sauce with a disc of baking parchment wrung out in cold water – this helps prevent a skin forming. Reheat the sauce before spooning it over the scallops.

You can grate the cheese and mix it with the herbs a couple of hours in advance. Actually searing the scallops takes very little time, as does the grilling of the cheese topping to the dish, so this is a convenient recipe to prepare, as well as being a delicious one to eat!

Scallops stir-fried with ginger and spring onions

This is so good, and so quick – yet because it is scallops, it is a main course of luxury! No salt is needed – the soy sauce will provide enough saltiness – and pepper is surplus to requirement in this dish, too.

Serves 6

3 tbsps olive oil
18 king scallops, with their roes
2 cloves of garlic, skinned and very finely chopped
12 spring onions, trimmed and sliced lengthways
about 2.5 cm/1 inch fresh ginger, skin pared off,
 and the ginger chopped finely
1 tbsp sesame oil
2 tbsps soy sauce
juice and finely grated rinds of 2 limes, well washed
 to remove preservative and dried before grating

Heat the olive oil in a large pan. With scissors, cut off the ridge of white muscle at the side of each scallop. Put the garlic, spring onions and ginger into the sauté pan over a moderate heat and cook for 2–3 minutes, then raise the heat a bit and add the scallops to the pan. Sauté them, turning after 30 seconds or so to cook on their other sides. When they turn opaque they are cooked. Add the sesame oil and the soy sauce to the pan, then the grated lime rinds and juice. Let all cook together for a minute, no more, then serve the scallops either whole, with the pan juices around them and a mixed leaf-and-herb salad at the side; or take each scallop and slice it diagonally into three slices. This dish is very good served cold if the weather is very hot.

main courses for special occasions

Steam-baked sea bass, with roast red peppers stuffed with cannellini beans, garlic, lemon, mint and parsley

This is so easy, delicious and convenient too. Unless you are feeding people with starch-demanding appetites, there really is no need for any more starch than is already there in the cannellini beans in the roast red peppers. A mixed-leaf salad is the only other possible requirement for this main course.

Serves 6

about 175 g/6 oz filleted sea bass per person
2 tbsps olive oil
juice of ½ lemon
½ tsp salt
a good grinding of black pepper

6 red peppers, cut in half and seeds scooped away *For the stuffed red*
4 tbsps olive oil *peppers*
1 red onion, skinned and diced finely
2 fat cloves of garlic, skinned and chopped finely
3 tins of cannellini beans, each weighing 400 g/15 oz
finely grated rind of 2 lemons, well washed to remove
preservative and dried before grating
2 tbsps chopped parsley and mint, mixed
½ tsp salt
a good grinding of black pepper
175 g/6 oz Parmesan, shaved (I use my potato peeler)

First make the stuffed red peppers. Rub the exterior of each pepper half with olive oil. Line a baking tray with a sheet of baking parchment and put the pepper halves on this.

Steam-baked sea bass, with roast red peppers stuffed with cannellini beans, garlic, lemon, mint and parsley

Heat 4 tablespoons of olive oil in a sauté pan and cook the diced onion in this for several minutes, then add the chopped garlic. Cook for 30 seconds and take the pan off the heat. Drain the brine from the canned cannellini beans, and run cold water through the drained beans in a large sieve. Pat the beans as dry as you can in the sieve, with kitchen paper, then mix the beans into the contents of the sauté pan, mixing thoroughly and adding the grated lemon rinds, parsley and mint. Season with salt and pepper. Divide this between each of the red pepper halves, and shave Parmesan over each. Bake in a moderate heat, 180°C/350°F/gas mark 4 (bottom-right oven in a four-door Aga), for 35–40 minutes.

Meanwhile, prepare the fish for baking by putting a sheet of baking parchment on a large baking tray. Put the filleted fish over the paper. Trickle olive oil and lemon juice scantily over the fish, and season with salt and pepper. Cover the fish with a sheet of baking parchment. Do this several hours in advance, if it is more convenient for you, but keep the baking tray in the fridge. Take it into room temperature 20 minutes before baking in a moderate heat, 180°C/350°F/gas mark 4 (bottom-right oven in a four-door Aga), for 20 minutes. Serve, accompanied by the stuffed red peppers.

main courses for special occasions

Baked fillets of sea bass with spinach, shallot and cumin timbales

These taste good and look pretty. I like to serve them with Sauce Bercy (page 268). And I love roast carrots and shallots as an accompanying vegetable, with well-beaten mashed potatoes containing either saffron strands or chopped parsley and chives, mixed. The mixture for the timbales can be made up a day in advance, but give the mixture a good stir before dividing it between the oiled moulds to bake the timbales. The timbales need to stand for 10–15 minutes after cooking, before being turned out at the side of the baked fish. You can either spoon the sauce over each, or hand it separately, whichever you choose.

Serves 6

12 sea bass fillets, each weighing about 75 g/3 oz
75 g/3 oz butter, cut into 12 bits

225 g/8 oz young spinach leaves *For the timbales*
150 ml/about ¼ pint near-boiling water
1 tsp whole cumin
2 tbsps olive oil
4 shallots, preferably the large, violet-fleshed type, skinned
and chopped, *or* 2 medium onions
1 clove of garlic, skinned and chopped
1 tsp flaky salt, preferably Maldon
a good grinding of black pepper
3 large eggs
1 tbsp lemon juice
300 ml/½ pint double cream

To make the timbale mixture, put the spinach into a large saucepan, add the nearly boiling water, cover the pan with its lid and put the pan on a high heat for barely 1 minute. The spinach will have wilted down. Drain it in a colander, and press it firmly to squeeze out all liquid from the spinach leaves. Chop the spinach in the colander, then put the chopped spinach into a food processor.

Baked fillets of sea bass with spinach, shallot and cumin timbales

Crush the cumin with a pestle in a mortar (or in a deep bowl with the end of a rolling pin) to release its flavour; buying whole spices and grinding them yourself gives far greater flavour than using ready-pulverized ones. Heat the olive oil in a sauté pan and fry the chopped shallots (or onions) with the cumin and garlic for several minutes over a moderate heat. The shallots should be quite soft. Season with salt and pepper, and put the contents of the sauté pan into the food processor with the spinach once the shallots have cooled. Whiz, adding the eggs, one by one. Lastly, briefly whiz in the lemon juice and the cream. Pour and scrape the mixture from the processor into a wide measure jug.

Rub 6 ramekins or moulds with olive oil. Divide the spinach mixture between them. Put the ramekins or moulds into a roasting tin and pour boiling water in to come halfway up the sides of the moulds. Bake in a moderate oven, 180°C/350°F/gas mark 4 (bottom-right oven in a four-door Aga), for 30–35 minutes, or until the tops of the timbales are quite firm and slightly puffed up. Take the roasting tin out of the oven and leave the timbales to stand for 10–15 minutes.

To cook the fish, line a baking tray or two with sheets of baking parchment. Put the pieces of sea bass on these, and put a small bit of butter on each. Cover with a second sheet of baking parchment and bake in a moderate heat, as for the timbales, once the timbales have been taken out of the oven, for 10–15 minutes. Check that the fish is cooked by gently forking into the thickest part of one of the fillets to see if it flakes. If it doesn't, cover the fish with the paper and continue to bake it for a further 5–10 minutes. This is what I call steam baking, because the fish steams between the paper yet it is also baked.

Run a knife around the inside of each timbale mould. Shake a timbale out on to each of six warmed plates, and put the cooked fish at the side of each.

main courses for special occasions

Shrimp puff pie

This is best made with the tiny brownish-pink shrimps that can only be found in Morecambe Bay and the Solway Firth. These are the shrimps which are potted and sealed with clarified butter. They have a slightly peppery taste, and I think they are unique. I grew up 15 miles from Morecambe Bay – sadly more synonymous these days with the tragic fate of the cockle-pickers. If you can't get these shrimps, use as good a quality prawn as you can buy. The mace is an essential seasoning in the sauce.

Serves 8

900 ml/1½ pints milk
1 small onion, skinned and halved
1 stick of celery, halved
1 blade of mace
a few black peppercorns
50 g/2 oz butter
50 g/2 oz flour
900 g/2 lb shrimps
freshly grated nutmeg
450 g/1 lb puff pastry
1 egg, beaten

Put the milk, onion, celery, mace and peppercorns in a saucepan over a gentle heat. Bring slowly to the boil, then draw the pan off the heat and leave to infuse for 30 minutes or so. Then strain the milk into a jug, ready for making into the sauce.

Melt the butter in a saucepan and stir in the flour. Cook for a couple of minutes, then stir in the reserved milk, stirring all the time until the sauce boils. Remove the pan from the heat and stir in the shrimps. Season with nutmeg. Pour into a greased pie dish.

Flour a working surface and roll out the pastry. Dampen the rim of the pie dish and cover the pie neatly. Cut 4–5 little slashes in the surface of the pie and decorate it with pastry trimmings. Brush with beaten egg. Bake in a hot oven, 200°C/400°F/gas mark 6 (top-right oven in a four-door Aga), for 35 minutes, or until the pastry is well-risen and golden brown.

Lemon sole, stuffed with squat lobsters, lemon, parsley and chives

Squat lobsters – squatties, colloquially to us in Skye – are such sweetly suc- culent shellfish. They are – rather grandly, I always think – referred to in the restaurant trade as langostinos. *But whatever you call them, they are a treat to eat and an enhancement to whatever they are cooked or served with. If you can't get squat lobsters, substitute the best type of prawns you can find. I love to serve (and eat!) this with any creamy sauce, either Sauce Bercy, Cream, Lemon and Chive Sauce, or Watercress and Lime Cream Sauce – to be found on pages 268, 265 and 272. Either very well mashed potatoes, or steamed new potatoes, whichever the season dictates, are the perfect accompaniment. And stir-fried or steamed sugarsnap peas are the only other requirement to make this an excellent main course for a special occasion.*

Serves 6

12 fillets of lemon sole, weighing in total
    about 1.2 kg/2½ lb
450 g/1 lb shelled squat lobsters (or prawns;
  if they are large, chop them)
2 tbsps olive oil
½ tsp salt
a good grinding of black pepper
a grating of nutmeg
juice and finely grated rind of 1 lemon, washed well to
    remove preservative and dried before grating
3 tbsps chopped parsley and snipped chives, mixed
75 g /3 oz butter, melted

Put a sheet of baking parchment on a baking tray. Have ready another sheet of parchment.

main courses for special occasions

In a bowl, mix together the squat lobsters (or prawns) with the olive oil, salt, pepper and nutmeg, lemon rind and juice and the parsley and chives. Mix all together very well.

Lay out the 12 fillets of lemon sole, and put a spoonful of the squat lobster mixture on one half of each fillet, dividing the mixture evenly between the 12 fillets. Fold the other bit of each fillet over the mixture, and put the folded-over stuffed fillets of fish on to the parchment on the baking tray. When you have completed this, brush each fillet with melted butter. Cover the butter-brushed fish with the remaining sheet of parchment, and bake in a moderate heat, 180°C/350°F/gas mark 4 (bottom-right oven in a four-door Aga), for 20–25 minutes.

You can prepare the fish for cooking several hours in advance, but keep it on the baking tray in the fridge until half an hour before cooking. Be sure to allow the tray and its contents a full 30 minutes at room temperature before baking, otherwise you will need a longer cooking time.

Fillets of lemon sole stuffed with salmon mousseline

This is an elegant main course for a special occasion. It is convenient, too, because it can be prepared several hours ahead of cooking. Stir-fried sugar-snap peas, with garlic and ginger, are good with this dish and Betty Allen's Noilly Prat Sauce (page 267) makes an excellent accompaniment.

Serves 6

6 fairly large fillets of lemon sole, each weighing
    about 175 g/6 oz, or 12 smaller ones
75 g/3 oz butter, cut into 6 bits (or 12, if you are cooking
    12 smaller fillets)

For the mousseline 450 g/1 lb organic salmon fillet, cut in chunks
2 anchovies, drained of their preserving oil
a good grinding of black pepper
150 ml/¼ pint double cream
1 large egg
1 large egg white
2 tbsps lemon juice
1 tbsp chopped parsley

Put the chunks of salmon into a food processor, with the anchovies, pepper, cream, egg and egg white, and whiz, adding the lemon juice and parsley. Scrape the contents of the processor into a bowl, and cover the bowl. Do this several hours ahead, if it is more convenient for you.

Assemble the lemon sole by dividing the salmon mousseline between the fillets, putting a spoonful on half of each fillet, and folding the other half over. Put them into a well-buttered ovenproof dish and put a piece of butter on each piece of fish. Cover with a sheet of baking parchment, and bake at a moderate heat, 180°C/350°F/gas mark 4 (bottom-right oven in a four-door Aga), for 20–25 minutes.

Serve this as soon as you can after it comes out of the oven, because it might become dry if it is kept warm for any length of time.

If you stuff the fish ahead of time and put the covered dish into the fridge for several hours, which you can perfectly well do, remember to take the dish into room temperature for half an hour before baking it, otherwise the cooking time won't be enough to cook the stuffed fish from its fridge chill.

Swordfish steaks, baked with lemon and dill, with cucumber and chilli salsa

This is so quick and easy to prepare – hours in advance of cooking if it is more convenient for you (but keep it covered, in the fridge). The salsa, too, actually benefits from advance preparation, because the time allows the flavours to mingle and settle down. And the slight crunch of the diced cucumber in the salsa gives a good contrasting texture to each mouthful.

You could substitute tuna for swordfish in this recipe.

Serves 6

6 swordfish steaks, each weighing about 175 g/6 oz
150 ml/¼ pint olive oil
juice and finely grated rind of 1 lemon, washed well
    to remove preservative and dried before grating
25 g/1 oz dill, torn in bits
½ tsp salt, preferably Maldon
a good grinding of black pepper

For the salsa   2 cucumbers
½ small red onion (use just ¼ if the onion is medium-sized)
2 sticks of celery, stringy bits removed
4 tomatoes
1 red chilli
2 tbsps olive oil
½ tsp salt
a good grinding of black pepper
1 tsp balsamic vinegar
2 tbsps chopped parsley

Peel the skin from the 2 cucumbers – I use a potato peeler: it takes seconds. Cut the cucumbers in half lengthwise and scoop away the

main courses for special occasions

seeds. Dice the cucumber evenly and small (if you have one, an onion dicer is ideal for this: it takes a minute to do both cucumbers, if that). Skin the onion and dice it so finely that it is almost minced. Slice the celery very thinly. Skin the tomatoes, cut them in quarters, throw away the seeds and dice the tomatoes about thumbnail size. Cut the chilli in half, discard the seeds and chop the chilli finely (wear rubber gloves to do this).

In a large bowl, mix together all the salsa ingredients thoroughly. Cover the bowl, and leave to stand for several hours.

Line a baking tray with a sheet of baking parchment, and have a second sheet ready to cover the fish when the steaks are prepared. Put the swordfish steaks on the parchment-lined tray.

In a measure jug, mix together the olive oil, lemon rind and juice, dill, salt and pepper. Spoon this over the steaks and cover with the second sheet of baking parchment. Either put the tray into the fridge for several hours, or bake straight away, in a moderate oven, 180°C/350°F/gas mark 4 (bottom-right oven in a four-door Aga), for 20 minutes.

Put a fish steak on each of six plates. Stir up the salsa and serve a spoonful or two alongside or on top of the fish steaks.

Beetroot and dill suèdoise with smoked trout, crème fraîche and horseradish

This makes a very good main course for a special occasion during the summer months. Alternatively, it can be made and served as a first course at any time of the year. Beware ever using pickled beetroot instead of whole, raw beetroot. I ate a beetroot something the other day in a fairly eminent restaurant and was astounded to taste that the beetroot had obviously been pickled. Disgusting!

A suèdoise is a jellied purée of either vegetables or fruit. It is fairly substantial, and the flavours of the beetroot suèdoise are delicious combined with the smoked trout and horseradish. Steamed new potatoes and a mixed-leaf salad are the other complementary accompaniments.

Don't worry about your hands being indelibly stained by preparing the beetroot – I promise, the stain will come off with one handwashing!

Serves 6

6 leaves of gelatine
150 ml/¼ pint hot stock (chicken or vegetable)
3 tbsps olive oil
2 shallots, skinned and chopped
6 raw beetroot, peeled and cut into quarters
600 ml/1 pint vegetable or chicken stock
juice of 1 lemon
½ tsp salt
a good grinding of black pepper
2 tbsps chopped dill
6 smoked trout
600 ml/1 pint full-fat crème fraîche
4 tsps best-quality horseradish dressing, preferably Isabella
    Massie or Moniack
2 tbsps chopped parsley and snipped chives, mixed

You can set the beetroot suèdoise either in a loaf tin, lined with cling-film, or in small individual moulds (teacups make ideal moulds) lined with clingfilm. I like to turn it out, so I shall assume that you will line a loaf tin or Pyrex terrine mould, capacity about 1.8 litres/3 pints, with clingfilm, pushing it right into the corners.

Soak the leaves of gelatine in cold water for at least 10 minutes, then drop them into the 150 ml/¼ pint hot stock.

Heat the olive oil in a saucepan and add the chopped shallots. Over moderate heat fry the shallots for 3–5 minutes, stirring to prevent sticking, until the shallots are transparent and soft. Add the quartered beetroot and continue to cook for a further few minutes before adding the 600 ml/1 pint stock. Cover the pan with its lid, and cook the contents over a moderate heat, with the stock simmering gently, until the biggest bit of beetroot is quite tender when stuck with a fork. Cool, and liquidize the contents of the pan till smooth, adding the lemon juice and the dissolved gelatine and stock. Season with salt and pepper, and mix in the chopped dill.

Pour the beetroot mixture into the lined loaf tin or mould and leave to set, for either several hours or overnight, in the fridge.

Flake the smoked trout into a bowl, carefully removing as many bones as you can, and all the skin. Add the crème fraîche, horse-radish, and chopped parsley and snipped chives, and mix all together well.

Turn out the suèdoise by inverting the terrine on to a serving plate, lifting off the terrine or loaf tin, and peeling off the clingfilm. Slice thickly to serve, with a spoonful of the smoked trout mixture beside each slice. Or you can spoon the flaked smoked trout in its dressing down either side of the turned-out suèdoise – the latter is good for a buffet table.

Marinated trout

You can use any freshwater fish instead of trout for this recipe. Alexandra, our eldest daughter, lives in the very middle of Austria and can only get fresh-water fish. We are so spoiled living in Skye, surrounded by sea: seafish is, I think, so varied and versatile, where freshwater fish is more limited. But I do love trout, and they have plenty of those in Austria! This is an elegant dish, and is good accompanied by well-beaten mashed potatoes, possibly containing saffron strands, and with a green vegetable, such as sugarsnap peas. The marinated trout have a creamy sauce made from the marinade, with a hint of ginger and lemon in the flavour.

Serves 6

6 tbsps olive oil
2 medium-sized onions, skinned and diced finely
a piece of root ginger, about 5 cm/2 inches in size, skin
    pared off and the ginger grated
2 tbsps chopped parsley
300 ml/½ pint dry white wine (I like to use a
    Sauvignon Blanc for this)
1 tsp salt, preferably Maldon
a good grinding of black pepper
6 trout
50 g/2 oz soft butter
2 tsps flour
300 ml/½ pint double cream
2 large egg yolks, beaten
1 tbsp lemon juice

Heat the olive oil in a sauté pan and fry the diced onions and grated ginger over a moderate heat for several minutes, until the onions are very soft. Cool, and then mix in the parsley. Mix in the white wine, salt and pepper.

main courses for special occasions

Put the trout into an ovenproof dish and cover with the onion and ginger mixture. Cover the dish and leave in a cool place, or in the fridge, for 3–4 hours. Turn the fish over in the marinade during this time. Remember to take the dish into room temperature for half an hour before baking.

Then bake the fish, with baking parchment covering the contents (not foil), in a moderate oven, temperature 180°C/350°F/gas mark 4 (bottom-right oven in a four-door Aga), for 30–35 minutes. Test a fish to see if it is done by gently forking into the fattest part. If it still looks a bit raw, cover the dish and continue cooking for a further 10 minutes.

When the trout are cooked, carefully drain the marinade and trout juices into a saucepan. Cover the cooked trout and keep them warm while you make the sauce. Melt the butter and stir the flour into it, mixing well. Heat the marinade, add the double cream and mix some of this hot sauce into the butter and flour mixture, mixing well. Scrape this into the contents of the saucepan and stir until the sauce bubbles. Let it boil for a couple of minutes, then draw the pan off the heat, mix some of the sauce into the 2 beaten egg yolks and then stir this back into the sauce within the pan. Stir, let the egg mixture cook in the heat of the sauce, but don't put the pan back on direct heat. Stir in the lemon juice, taste and check for seasoning, adding more salt and pepper if you think it is needed. Pour the sauce over the trout, and serve.

Devilled seafood

Now this recipe hails from my youth, when my father was stationed in Norfolk, Virginia, and we lived in Virginia Beach. My parents loved our years spent living in other countries, and they always made the most of wherever we lived. Virginia was no exception, and we made many lifelong friends there. This recipe was given to my mother by one of them, and has featured at parties on occasion ever since. I do agree with those of you who, on reading the list of ingredients, are slightly incredulous. It seems strange that a delicious taste could result from the amalgamation of these ingredients, but it does, I promise you! In this version I have put less flour than is in the original, which used to be rather stiff of texture. I urge you to try it: it really is good, and it can be made several hours, even a day, in advance. But it must, of course, be kept in the fridge.

Use any of cod, hake, monkfish, ling, megrim or whiting for this dish. The shellfish could be crab, scallops and prawns. Cut large scallops into 3 bits; they will cook in the sauce as the dish reheats. Alternatively, you can, if you wish, cook them with the fish, as in the method.

Serves 8

900 g/2 lb firm-fleshed white fish
450 g/1 lb shellfish
milk, to cook the fish

For the sauce 225 g/8 oz butter
8 level tbsps flour
300 ml/½ pint evaporated milk
300 ml/½ pint beef consommé
1 tbsp lemon juice
1 tbsp Worcester sauce
4 tbsps Heinz tomato ketchup
1 tbsp good-quality (not harshly vinegary) creamy
    horseradish sauce
1 fat garlic clove, skinned and chopped
1 rounded tsp English mustard
1 tsp salt

1 tsp strong soy sauce
a dash of Tabasco
4 tbsps chopped parsley
300 ml/½ pint sherry

110 g/4 oz fresh brown or white breadcrumbs
approx. 75 g/3 oz butter, cut into small bits

Put the white fish on to a board, feel it and remove any bones or skin. Cut the fish into bite-sized pieces, about 4 cm (1½ inches). Put the fish and any uncooked shellfish into a saucepan with milk to cover. Bring the milk to simmer, then take the pan off the heat and cool the fish in the milk.

Make the sauce by melting the butter in a large saucepan. Stir in the flour and cook for a couple of minutes. Gradually add all the other ingredients except the bits of butter, stirring till the sauce boils. Once it has boiled, take the pan off the heat.

Strain the cooked fish, reserving the milk to make into a fish soup in the near future.

Mix the barely cooked pieces of fish and the shellfish into the sauce. Pour the contents of the saucepan into a large ovenproof dish. Sprinkle breadcrumbs over the surface, and dot with the bits of butter.

Reheat by baking the dish in a moderate oven, 180°C/350°F/gas mark 4 (bottom-right oven in a four-door Aga), for 25–30 minutes, or until the crumbs are browned and the sauce is bubbling around the edges. Serve this with boiled basmati rice, and with a green vegetable – courgettes or green beans.

Shellfish, cream and brandy stew

You can vary the shellfish content of this recipe according to what you like and what you can get. This is a deeply decadent and utterly delicious main course for a special occasion. I like it best served with boiled basmati rice with lots of chopped parsley and snipped chives mixed through it, and with a mixed-leaf salad.

For instructions on cooking shellfish, see pages 20–22. Remember to discard any mussels that remain shut after cooking.

Serves 6–8

1 cooked lobster, weighing about 700 g/1½ lb,
    flesh cut into chunks
8 large scallops, cooked and cut in half
225 g/8 oz cooked, shelled prawns
225 g/8 oz white crabmeat
575 ml/1 pint mussels in their shells,
    cooked then taken out of their shells

For the sauce 75 g/3 oz butter
2 medium onions, skinned and
    finely chopped
2 tsps curry powder
1 rounded tbsp flour
300 ml/½ pint double cream
6 tbsps brandy
salt
freshly ground black pepper
1 heaped tbsp finely chopped parsley

main courses for special occasions

First make the sauce. Melt the butter in a large saucepan. Add the onion and cook for 5 minutes until it is soft and transparent. Stir in the curry powder and flour, and cook for a further couple of minutes. Then pour in the cream, stirring all the time until the sauce is simmering gently. Take the pan off the heat and stir in the brandy. Season to taste.

Add the cooked shellfish and reheat, stirring carefully so as not to break them up, until the sauce is just barely simmering once more. Tip the contents of the saucepan into a warmed serving dish, sprinkle with the chopped parsley and serve.

Seafood mayonnaise

The sauce for this recipe is so simple and quick, but it is so delicious. It makes a perfect main course for a party, when doubled or trebled in amounts. I'm sure that it is the combination of smoked and unsmoked fish which is the secret to the success of this recipe. You can use any shellfish you choose. When I say 'good' mayonnaise, in the list of ingredients, I really mean home-made, because only home-made is really good! Serve boiled basmati rice, cooled, with the seafood mayonnaise, but mix the cooked rice with olive oil, lemon rind and juice and snipped chives to make it look more interesting as well as taste good. Any green leafy salad, combining any of the wide variety of leaves obtainable these days, is the only other accompaniment necessary, except, possibly, a tomato salad as well!

Serves 6

450 g/1 lb smoked haddock
450 g/1 lb firm-fleshed white fish – cod, hake, megrim, for instance
225g/8 oz prawns or mussels (or a combination of both), cooked
150 ml/¼ pint double cream, whipped
300 ml/½ pint good mayonnaise
1 tbsp lemon juice
1 rounded tsp medium-strength curry powder
50 g/2 oz tinned anchovies, drained, patted dry with
    kitchen paper, and chopped finely
2 tbsps chopped parsley and snipped chives, mixed
a dash of Tabasco

Feel the fish all over, on a board, and remove any bones your fingertips encounter. Cut the fish into bite-sized bits, about 2.5 cm/1 inch in size. Cover a roasting tin with a sheet of baking parchment and put the pieces of fish on this. Cover with a second sheet of parchment, pressing it down over the fish. Bake in a moderate oven, 180°C/350°F/gas mark 4 (bottom-right oven in a four-door Aga), for

main courses for special occasions

15–20 minutes. Check that it is cooked by forking into the thickest part of one of the pieces of fish. If it still looks a bit undercooked for your liking, re-cover the fish and bake for a further 5 minutes. When cooked, take the roasting tin out of the oven and cool, still covered with paper – this helps prevent the surface of the fish drying out as it cools.

In a very large mixing bowl, combine the whipped cream with the mayonnaise, lemon juice, curry powder, chopped anchovies, herbs and Tabasco. Carefully mix in the cooled, cooked fish and shellfish – carefully, so as not to break up the pieces of fish more than you can help.

Spoon the fish and shellfish mayonnaise on to a serving dish.

Sauces, salsas accompanim

Cold sauces

s and
ts

Hot sauces

Accompaniments

THE SAUCES IN THIS CHAPTER ARE DIVIDED IN TWO SECTIONS: cold and hot. Occasionally a sauce can be served either hot or cold – as in the case of the Roast Red Pepper Sauce – so I have chosen to put it in the cold section. The various recipes which aren't sauce or salsa include one for Melba toast; it will seem faintly ridiculous even to include it in this book, but you wouldn't imagine how often I am asked how it is made. And it is so convenient, too, because it can be made days – even weeks – in advance, providing that it is kept in an airtight container. Anchovy sablés aren't a sauce or a salsa, either, yet they can be a delicious savoury, or are useful to serve along with drinks: a type of canapé.

In many cases a sauce can be made well in advance. The fish is so simply cooked and the sauce embellishes and enhances it, but at the cook's convenience. Taste is a very individual thing, and we all like to adjust the seasonings in what we eat. But it goes much further than how much or how little salt and pepper we like. We all like different amounts of lemon juice or wine vinegar in sauces, so do add more or use less of any flavouring according to how you like to eat. Some people abhor the idea of including sugar amongst the ingredients of mayonnaise, but I always add caster sugar to both my mayonnaise and my vinaigrette dressings. How small you dice fruit and vegetables for a salsa is really up to you. I tend to describe size either by thumbnail or I say 'very finely', which is smaller; but if you like a chunkier-textured salsa, then by all means slice and dice the content in larger bits.

The main purpose of the recipes in this chapter, whether hot or cold, is to make eating the fish or shellfish even better – and conveniently, too.

Cold sauces

Mayonnaise

We are lucky to get our eggs from 2 miles away and they are the best eggs, I do believe. The yolks are so orange that our mayonnaise looks deeply, impressively delicious – and that is before it is tasted. It is deep gold in colour, almost as though it contained saffron, but the colour comes entirely from the depth of hue of the yolks.

Mayonnaise is such a versatile sauce, just as delicious with hot food as with cold. It comes in all sorts of flavours and variations, and following the basic recipe I suggest several of these. One of the most bastardized must be tartare sauce, which is mayonnaise with delicious additions, yet this sauce is purveyed by fast-food outlets in small foil containers tasting of nothing but malt vinegar. Far too many people associate tartare sauce with the taste of vinegar and with nothing else, yet this sauce is almost a meal in itself and is a wonderful accompaniment for simply cooked fillets of fish of all types.

For making basic mayonnaise, I use a second pressing oil, which is a lighter oil. If you find all olive oil too heavy for your taste, try using half olive and half sunflower or grapeseed oil.

**Serves 6
(generously)**

1 large egg
2 egg yolks
1 level tsp salt, preferably Maldon
lots of ground black pepper
1 tsp caster sugar
1 rounded tsp Dijon mustard
450 ml/¾ pint olive oil
1 tbsp lemon juice
2 tbsps white wine vinegar

sauces, salsas and accompaniments

Break the egg into a food processor and add the 2 egg yolks. Add the salt, pepper, sugar and Dijon mustard and whiz, adding the oil drop by drop until you have a thick emulsion, then continue to add the oil in a thin, steady trickle. When all the oil is incorporated, add the lemon juice and white wine vinegar. Taste, and add more vinegar if you think the mayonnaise tastes a bit bland. If the mayonnaise is too thick for your liking, whiz in 1–2 tablespoons of nearly boiling water, which thins it down slightly. Scrape the contents of the processor into a bowl, cover with clingfilm and store the mayonnaise in the fridge; it will keep for up to 5 days.

Tartare sauce

2 tbsps chopped parsley
2 hardboiled eggs, chopped finely
2 tsps fat capers, chopped
about 2 tbsps best black olives (I prefer Kalamata olives),
flesh cut from stones
2 gherkins, chopped (optional)
⅓ of a cucumber, peeled, cut lengthways,
seeded and diced finely
1 batch of mayonnaise (page 250)

Fold all the ingredients into the mayonnaise.

Tomato and garlic mayonnaise

3 tomatoes
1–2 fat cloves of garlic
1 batch of mayonnaise (page 250)

Put the tomatoes on the end of a fork and plunge them into boiling water for enough seconds to let the skin start peeling away from the fork prongs. Take the tomatoes out and peel off their skins. Cut each in quarters and scoop away the seeds – this is essential, because if left in the seeds seep liquid, which will make the mayonnaise runny. Chop the tomato flesh into thumbnail-size dice.

Skin and finely chop the garlic, then fold it and the diced tomato flesh through the mayonnaise. If you like, add some torn basil leaves. This mayonnaise is very good with hot salmon, however it is cooked – barbecued, baked or seared – or with cold poached salmon.

sauces, salsas and accompaniments

Slightly curried mayonnaise

I love this mayonnaise, especially with white fish coated in nuts and fried, but it is good with any type of fish or shellfish.

2 tsps runny honey
1 rounded tsp medium-strength curry powder
1 batch of mayonnaise (page 250)

Work together the honey and curry powder in a bowl, gradually adding a spoonful of mayonnaise and working that in. After 3 spoonfuls of mayonnaise (I use a tablespoon) the mixture should be easy to stir into the rest of the mayonnaise.

Cucumber and dill mayonnaise

75 g/3 oz dill, chopped
½ cucumber, peeled, cut lengthways, seeded and diced small
1 batch of mayonnaise (page 250)

Fold the dill and diced cucumber through the mayonnaise. This is good with all types of plain cooked fish which has no other sauce. It is particularly good with softer-fleshed fish, such as plaice, lemon sole or skate – as opposed to firm-fleshed fish like monkfish or tuna – because the texture of the diced cucumber is a very good contrast to soft fish.

Chive, parsley and Dijon vinaigrette

This is very good spooned over baked fish, like sea bass, cod, hake or whiting. Serve the fish warm, so that it absorbs the flavours of the dressing. The dressing can be made a day in advance.

Serves 6

3 tbsps chopped parsley and snipped chives, mixed

2 tsps Dijon mustard

1 tsp caster sugar

1 level tsp salt

a good grinding of black pepper

300 ml/½ pint olive oil

finely grated rind of 1 lemon, well washed to remove
preservative and dried before grating

3 tbsps lemon juice

Mix together all the ingredients very well. If you make it in advance, be sure to mix it up very well again before spooning it over the baked, cooked fish.

Horseradish, apple and crème fraîche dressing

This is so simple, yet so very good with all types of hot-smoked fish, most notably with hot-smoked trout and salmon. I use a very coarse grater for the apples. Avoid harsh, vinegary horseradish sauces; good brands are Moniack or Isabella Massie's.

Serves 6

3 good eating apples
450 ml/¾ pint crème fraîche
1 tbsp creamy horseradish sauce

Peel, quarter and core the apples, then grate them. You can, if you prefer, peel the apples whole and grate them, but do watch out not to include any of the core!

Stir together all the ingredients and serve with either plain hot-smoked salmon or trout fillets, or with any dish that includes these fish in any form.

Tomato and horseradish cream

This is a sauce deliciously suitable for serving as an accompaniment to any cold fish, shellfish or smoked fish, or you can use it for coating the fish. I first realized just what made the sauce served with shrimp in America so hot and good – horseradish. My sauce is a rather more in-depth version – but the two basic ingredients, tomatoes and horseradish, owe everything to American inspiration.

My favourite horseradish sauce is made by Moniack or by Isabella Massie. Only Heinz tomato ketchup will do. If you wonder why, read the ingredients in Heinz, compare them to other brands and you will understand!

Serves 6

450 ml/¾ pint crème fraîche
2 heaped tsps creamy horseradish sauce
1 tbsp Heinz tomato ketchup
1 clove of garlic, skinned and chopped very finely
1 rounded tsp Dijon mustard

Mix all the ingredients together several hours in advance of eating – this lets the flavours settle down together. Cover the bowl with cling-film and keep it in the fridge till 20 minutes or so before serving.

Roast red pepper and balsamic vinegar sauce

This is good with any type of fish, however the fish is cooked, but it is above all else utterly delicious with chargrilled monkfish!

Serves 6

6 red peppers
300 ml/½ pint olive oil
2 tsps balsamic vinegar
½ tsp salt
lots of black pepper

Cut each pepper in half, remove the seeds and lay the peppers skin uppermost on a baking tray under a hot grill till the skin forms black blisters. Remove from the baking tray and put the pepper halves into a polythene bag. Leave for 10 minutes.

Peel the skin from the peppers after their rest in the polythene bag. Put the pepper halves into a food processor and whiz, adding the olive oil in a very thin trickle. Whiz in the balsamic vinegar, and season with salt and pepper. Serve this sauce warm or cold.

Options: you can fold this mixture into 150 ml/¼ pint of crème fraîche if you wish, or into the same amount of mayonnaise. In both cases the sauce must then be served cold.

sauces, salsas and accompaniments

Black olive relish

This is really Tapenade, a sort of pâté of olives. It is good with chargrilled monkfish, or with any barbecued or chargrilled fish or shellfish. It keeps, with a film of olive oil covering it, in a screw-topped jar in the fridge for several weeks. Serve in teaspoon-sized quenelle shapes, 2–3 per person.

Serves 6

30 best-quality black olives (for me this means Kalamata olives)
1 clove of garlic, skinned
2 anchovy fillets, drained of their preserving oil
300 ml/½ pint olive oil
2 tbsps lemon juice
lots of black pepper (no need for salt: the anchovies
and olives are salty enough)
1 tbsp chopped parsley

Cut the flesh from the stones of the olives and throw the stones away. Put the olive flesh into a food processor with the garlic and the anchovies. Whiz to a paste, then add the olive oil in a thin trickle, and lastly the lemon juice. Season with black pepper. Stir in the chopped parsley just before serving.

Avocado salsa

This is excellent with any type of fish or shellfish, whether the fish is to be served hot or cold. In sufficient amounts this salsa is much more than a garnish-cum-taste sample: it is a vegetable accompaniment too (and the recipe is for just that – not for a mere teaspoonful at the side). You can vary the ingredients according to your tastes: for instance, leave out the small amount of red onion and the garlic if you dislike them.

Serves 6

3 avocados, preferably the dark-skinned knobbly variety
2 red peppers
6 tomatoes, skinned, seeded and diced small and neatly
about 50 g/2 oz coriander, chopped coarsely
1 fat clove of garlic, skinned and chopped finely
½ a small red onion, skinned and diced very finely and neatly
juice and finely grated rind of 1 lime, well washed
   to remove preservative and dried before grating
3 tbsps olive oil
½ tsp salt, preferably Maldon
a good grinding of black pepper

Cut each red pepper in half, scoop out and throw away the seeds. Slice the flesh into small, neat dice – this is easy if, like us, you have an onion dicer, which dices everything else as well as onions!

Cut each avocado in half, flick out the stones, peel and then chop the flesh into thumbnail-size dice.

Put the diced peppers into a mixing bowl with the diced avocados, tomatoes, coriander, garlic, red onion, lime rind and juice, olive oil, salt and pepper. Carefully – so as not to crush the diced avocado flesh – mix all together thoroughly.

This can be made 2–3 hours before serving, but cover the ingredients of the bowl closely with clingfilm to help prevent discolouring.

Hot sauces

Hollandaise sauce

This is almost as variable in potential content as mayonnaise. It is a myth that hollandaise sauce is difficult to make, or that it must be made at the last minute. If I can make it with ease, anyone else can too! And as for last minute, hollandaise sauce can be made hours ahead and kept warm in a Thermos flask.

How you sharpen the flavour is up to you: either use lemon juice, which is good with all types of fish and shellfish, or reduce white wine vinegar with a few slices of raw onion, some celery, some fennel (if you have any), a bay leaf, parsley stalks (crushed to release more flavour from them), black peppercorns and salt. When the amount of vinegar has reduced by half – I use a whole bottle – leave the contents of the saucepan to cool completely then strain the vinegar into a jug, pour it into a screw-topped jar and store it in the fridge, to reheat in small amounts when you are making hollandaise sauce. It gives much more depth of taste.

There are two ways to make hollandaise sauce; I give them both below. If you want to increase the quantity, just add another yolk and 50 g/2 oz butter for every 2 people.

Serves 6

3 large egg yolks
175 g/6 oz butter (we use Lurpak), cut into 6 bits
2–3 tbsps either lemon juice *or* reduced
white wine vinegar (see above), heated

First method: put the yolks into a Pyrex bowl over a saucepan containing gently simmering water. With a small whisk, stir the yolks well, then, as the bowl heats, stir in the butter a piece at a time, adding the next bit once the previous bit has melted and become incorporated into the sauce. You should very soon form a thick emulsion between the yolks and butter in the bowl. When all the butter is used up, stir in the heated lemon juice or wine vinegar, take the bowl off the heat, and you should have a sauce resembling custard in appearance. The depth of colour of the sauce will depend on the eggs you use – our eggs are local and have very deep golden yolks, so our hollandaise and mayonnaise sauces are a wonderful deep yellow in colour.

Should the sauce appear to be curdling at any point during its making, remove the bowl from the pan of water under it and beat the contents like mad. If further action is needed, scrape the sauce into a clean, cold bowl and beat. Yet further action can be taken by beating in a spoonful or two of the hot water from the pan. Ninety-nine times out of a hundred a curdling hollandaise sauce is redeemable, so take heart – but if the water is only gently simmering, it really shouldn't ever be a problem.

The other method of making hollandaise sauce is how we make it in the hotel kitchen for our guests, and you may prefer to do it this way, too, for smaller numbers.

Put the butter into a saucepan over a moderate heat to melt and become foaming hot. Put the yolks into a food processor and whiz, adding the very hot melted butter in a thin, steady stream. Lastly, whiz in the heated lemon juice or reduced wine vinegar.

If you make the sauce half an hour ahead, just take the bowl from the saucepan (or scrape the contents from the food processor bowl into a bowl) and put the bowl in a warm place – at the back of the Aga, if you have one, is ideal. A thin skin will form on the surface which stirs in easily. Alternatively, pour the hot sauce into a Thermos flask and screw on the top.

Below are two variations on the basic hollandaise recipe.

Tomato and basil sauce

3 tomatoes, skinned, halved, seeded and flesh diced
50 g/2 oz basil leaves, torn up
1 batch of hollandaise (page 261)

Mix the tomatoes and basil into the hollandaise. This is particularly
good with salmon.

Orange and tomato sauce

finely grated rind of 2 oranges, thoroughly washed and dried before grating
2 tsps tomato purée
1 batch of hollandaise (page 261)

Stir the orange rind and tomato purée into the hollandaise sauce,
mixing thoroughly. This is good with all types of fish.

Tomato and chilli sauce

A tomato sauce can be all-encompassing – it can contain two or three vegetables as well as the tomatoes, as in this recipe, and the chilli just lifts the sauce. This is so good nutritionally, as well as being full of taste and complementary to all types of baked or grilled fish. It freezes excellently.

Serves 6

3 tbsps olive oil
2 onions, skinned and diced finely
2 sticks celery, trimmed of stringy bits and sliced finely
1–2 cloves of garlic, skinned and chopped finely
2 tins chopped tomatoes, each weighing 400 g/15 oz
½ tsp dried chilli flakes
½ tsp salt
½ tsp caster sugar (to counteract any slight bitterness from the tomato seeds)
a good grinding of black pepper

Heat the olive oil and fry the finely diced onions and sliced celery until the onions are quite soft and transparent-looking. Add the chopped garlic and the contents of the tins of tomatoes, and stir in the chilli flakes, salt, sugar and pepper. Let this sauce reach simmering point and simmer gently for 5–7 minutes. Either serve as it is, or cool and liquidize to a velvety smoothness, then reheat to serve. Because the onions are neatly diced and the celery finely sliced, the sauce looks good even if you decide not to liquidize it. It can be made 3 days in advance, but it must be kept in a covered bowl in the fridge.

Cream, lemon and chive sauce

This is the simplest sauce of all, and I repeat it here because so very many people have told me that they love it as it tastes so good for so little input on the part of the cook. It embellishes every type of fish and shellfish that I can think of.

Serves 6

600 ml/1 pint double cream
juice and finely grated rind of 1 lemon, washed well to
remove preservative and dried before grating
75 g/3 oz chives, snipped very small with scissors
½ tsp salt
a good grinding of black pepper

Put the cream into a saucepan over a moderate heat and simmer till thick and yellow – its colour deepens as it cooks. Don't be tempted to try this sauce with any cream less high in fat content than double – it just won't thicken and it may well split, or curdle. Double is essential! When the cream is as thick as you want, add the lemon rind and juice, the snipped chives, and the salt and pepper. Serve.

Leek and ginger sauce

This is delicious, as low in fat as the creamy lemon and chive one is high, and the leeks and ginger are so good with robust white-fleshed fish such as cod, hake, monkfish or whiting.

Serves 6

3 tbsps olive oil
6 good-sized leeks (9 small), washed, trimmed of outer
   leaves and sliced very thinly
8-cm/3-inch piece of fresh ginger, skin pared off and the
   ginger chopped finely or coarsely grated
juice and finely grated rind of 1 lemon, washed well
   to remove preservative and dried before grating
½ tsp salt, preferably Maldon
a good grinding of black pepper

Heat the oil in a large sauté pan and fry the sliced leeks and ginger together for several minutes. The leeks look a sizeable amount for a sauce, but as they cook they wilt down, and the ginger becomes much gentler of taste than when it is raw. When the leeks are quite soft and collapsed, stir in the lemon rind and juice, and the salt and pepper. Either serve, or cool and reheat to serve.

sauces, salsas and accompaniments

Betty Allen's Noilly Prat sauce

Betty Allen, who with her husband Eric used to run the wonderful Airds Hotel at Port Appin, in Argyllshire, gave me this recipe many years ago. She is a most marvellous cook. She and her husband now live at and run the Kinloch House Hotel with their son Graeme and his wife Anne, so in a way they and we are alike, in that we live and work with our daughter Isabella and her husband Tom, here at this Kinloch, Kinloch Lodge in Skye!

The amount below gives a small spoonful suitable to serve with a hot fish mousse or fish first course. Just double the amount if the sauce is to accompany a main course fish for 6 people.

Serves 6

1 slice of onion, *or* ½ shallot, skinned
4 tbsps Noilly Prat
125 ml/4 fl. oz fish stock
150 ml/¼ pint double cream
50 g/2 oz butter, cut into 6 pieces
a good pinch of salt
a good grinding of black pepper

Put the piece of shallot or onion into a saucepan with the Noilly Prat and the fish stock. Boil until the amount is reduced by half. Then stir in the cream and boil again to thicken and reduce a bit, until the sauce is the thickness of pouring cream. Strain, and whisk the butter into the strained sauce, a piece at a time, until the sauce is glossy and creamy. Season with salt and pepper. Spoon over or around a mousse or timbale, or beside steamed fish or shellfish for a first course.

Sauce Bercy

I don't remember where Pete, with whom I've worked for the past 32 years and who is such a good friend, and I found this sauce. We have been making it over the past three decades here at Kinloch and it is very good indeed with all types of fish and shellfish, or with a mixture of both.

Serves 6

3 shallots, skinned and very finely diced (almost minced)
150 ml/¼ pint dry white wine
150 ml/¼ pint fish or vegetable stock
110 g/4 oz butter, cut into 6 bits
1 tbsp lemon juice
¼ tsp salt, preferably Maldon
a good grinding of black pepper
1 tbsp chopped parsley

Put the shallots into a saucepan with the wine and stock. Simmer this until the liquid has reduced by half. Then whisk in the butter, a piece at a time. Whisk in the lemon juice, take the pan off the heat, and season with salt and pepper. This will keep hot but not on direct heat. Stir in the chopped parsley just before serving. Serve warm.

Horseradish and parsley sauce messine

This is rather less rich than hollandaise sauce (see page 261) and equally good with baked or grilled fish of all varieties. My favourite horseradish sauces are made by Moniack and by Isabella Massie.

Serves 6

300 ml/½ pint single cream
50 g/2 oz butter
1 tsp flour
2 egg yolks
1 tsp mustard powder
a pinch of salt
a good grinding of black pepper
juice and finely grated rind of 1 lemon, washed well to
remove preservative and dried before grating
2 tsps creamy horseradish sauce
1 tbsp chopped parsley

Put the cream, butter, flour, egg yolks, mustard, salt and pepper into a blender or food processor and whiz till smooth. Pour this mixture into a Pyrex bowl and add the grated lemon rind – not yet the juice. Put the bowl over a saucepan of simmering water and stir from time to time until the sauce thickens to the consistency of thick cream. Mix in the lemon juice and horseradish, and, just before serving, add the chopped parsley. The sauce can be kept warm in the bowl over the pan of simmering water. Unlike hollandaise sauce, this won't curdle as it sits over the heat.

Brown butter, lemon and caper sauce

This is one of my favourites. I love the nutty taste of brown butter, and I love this sauce with either skate or halibut, and with pretty well all other types of fish too. But the sauce's delicious rating depends entirely on the quality of the capers used. The average, catering-type caper is a miserable, tiny, vinegar-harsh thing beneath contemplation. You can buy plump and juicy capers – the best are those preserved in olive oil – but they are difficult to find. So buy best-quality capers, drain off their wine-vinegar brine and, in a sieve, run cold water through the capers gently: if the water runs with force, it smashes the capers against the mesh of the sieve. Run water through them for about 5 minutes. Then drain as well as you can, pat them dry with kitchen paper and put them into a jam jar. Fill the jar with olive oil, cover and leave for at least 2 days before using. Store them in the fridge – the oil will become cloudy and solid, but still it imparts flavour and texture to the capers.

Serves 6

225 g/8 oz butter (we use Lurpak)
finely grated rind of 1 lemon, washed well to
   remove preservative and dried before grating
a good grinding of black pepper (no salt:
   the capers add enough of their own)
2 tbsps lemon juice
4 tsps capers (see above), drained of their olive oil

Melt the butter in a saucepan. Let it cook over a moderate heat until it begins to turn brown – it is the milky part in the butter which turns brown and nutty tasting. This takes several minutes, but don't be tempted to turn up the heat because you will then burn the butter – a quite different thing.

Once the butter has browned, add the lemon rind and black pepper, the lemon juice and capers, and keep the sauce warm till you are ready to serve it, spooned over the fish. If you like, you can also add a tablespoon of chopped parsley.

Shallot, white wine and saffron cream sauce

This is such a convenient sauce, it goes deliciously with everything – all types of fish, as well as with dishes like Coulibiac of salmon. You can make this sauce a day in advance, keep it in the fridge and reheat it before serving. It is also very good with kedgeree (as is hollandaise sauce – see page 261). On no account be tempted to use anything other than saffron strands, the real thing.

Serves 6

50 g/2 oz butter
2 shallots, skinned and very finely chopped
300 ml/½ pint fish or vegetable stock
150 ml/¼ pint white wine
2 good pinches saffron strands
juice and grated rind of 1 lemon, washed well to remove
preservative and dried before grating
300 ml/½ pint double cream
½ tsp salt, preferably Maldon
a good grinding of black pepper

Melt the butter in a saucepan and fry the diced shallots over a moderate heat until they are really soft. Add the stock, white wine and saffron strands and simmer till the liquid has reduced by just more than half in amount. Add the lemon rind and juice and simmer for a further couple of minutes.

Stir in the double cream – it must be double because any lesser fat content (such as whipping or single cream) will tend to curdle and it won't thicken. Let the sauce bubble until it is the texture of thick cream. Season with salt and pepper. The sauce will be a deep, glorious orangey-yellow colour, with the subtle flavour from the saffron.

Watercress and lime cream sauce

Watercress varies so much in its strength. Our watercress is grown here in Skye and it has a much more distinctly peppery taste than any of the good but rather dull commercially grown watercress sold in bags in supermarkets up and down the country. This sauce is very good with all types of firm-fleshed white fish, whether baked or grilled.

Serves 6

50 g/2 oz butter
1 onion, *or* 2 shallots, skinned and diced
300 ml/½ pint chicken or fish stock
300 ml/½ pint double cream
juice and finely grated rind of 1 lime, washed well to
    remove preservative and dried before grating
½ tsp salt
a good grinding of black pepper
50 g/2 oz watercress, steamed till just wilted

Melt the butter in a saucepan. Add the diced onion or shallots and sauté in the melted butter for 2–3 minutes before adding the stock. Simmer gently until the stock has virtually evaporated. Add the cream and simmer, stirring, till thickened – about 2 minutes' fast boiling. Take the pan off the heat, add the lime rind and juice, salt and pepper, then put the sauce and the watercress into a food processor and whiz till smooth. Scrape the sauce back into the saucepan from the processor bowl. Reheat gently to serve.

Glyn's sweet chilli sauce

Glyn Musker is a chef who came to work with us in 2005 and who has become very much one of us here at Kinloch. This sauce, his recipe, is one of the best things to eat with seared scallops – in fact it is the best thing, according to so many of our guests, and us! It can be made several days in advance and kept in the fridge. It becomes quite thickly sticky in the fridge, but don't worry – it relaxes on warming through. We serve a spoonful of thick crème fraîche with each serving of seared scallops and sweet chilli sauce.

4 large red chillies, ends cut off

10 cloves of garlic, peeled and chopped

3 thumbs of fresh root ginger, skin cut off and the ginger chopped

1 thumb of galangal (I use Steenberg's Galangal, 3 tsps)

8 lime leaves

3 stems lemongrass, cut into bits

75 g/3 oz coriander

450 ml caster sugar (measure in a measure jug)

4 tbsps water

100 ml/3 fl. oz cider or white wine vinegar

1 tbsp Asian fish sauce (Nam Pla)

1 tbsp tamarind

Put the chillies, chopped (seeds and all), into a food processor with the chopped garlic and ginger, the galangal, lime leaves, lemongrass bits and the coriander. Whiz to a paste.

Put the sugar in the water in a pan, gently heat and stir until the sugar has dissolved entirely before letting it boil. Boil for 3 minutes.

Mix the paste, scraped from the processor, into the strong sugar syrup and stir in the vinegar, fish sauce and tamarind. Simmer for 3 minutes.

Accompaniments

Melba toast

I refer so often throughout the first-course chapter to Melba toast – a perfect accompaniment to a pâté, salad, or creamy fish or shellfish first course – that I thought I must repeat the recipe in this book, although it hardly counts as a recipe, it is so easy and straightforward. The only essentials are to watch the toasting bread as it curls up to check that it doesn't burn, and to let the finished Melba toast triangles cool completely before storing them. Melba toast not only adds a delicious contrasting crunchy texture, which is so useful with smooth-textured pâtés, but it is also very convenient, in that it can be made many days in advance, providing that it is kept in an absolutely airtight container. In fact, I once found some Melba toast left over on the top shelf of my larder which had been there for 9 weeks, and it tasted perfectly fine!

Serves 6

12 slices from a medium-sliced loaf, either white or brown

Cut the crusts off the bread and toast each slice. With a sharply serrated bread knife, carefully slice each toasted slice in half, leaving you with two thin slices, toasted on one side, the other side bread. Under a red-hot grill, toast the bread side of each slice until it curls up and is crisply golden brown. Cool each curly slice of Melba toast, then store in an airtight tin.

sauces, salsas and accompaniments

Anchovy sablés

These are very rich and fragile biscuits, and the cheese and anchovy content makes them quite delicious. They can be made in advance, cooled and stored in a solid polythene bag for 2 days, or they can be frozen.

Makes about 16

110 g/4 oz butter
110 g/4 oz plain flour
110 g/4 oz grated Parmesan cheese
1 tsp anchovy paste – Gentleman's Relish (Patum Peperium)
1 egg, beaten

Put all the ingredients into a food processor and whiz to a ball of dough. Lightly flour a work surface and a rolling pin, and roll out the dough to a thickness of about ½ cm/⅛ inch. Cut into small rounds, about 2 cm/¾ inch in diameter, and put them on a baking sheet. Brush each with beaten egg. Bake in a hot oven, 200°C/400°F/gas mark 6 (top-right oven in a four-door Aga), for 7–10 minutes – set the timer; the biscuits should be golden brown and crisp. Let them stand on the baking tray for a minute before carefully lifting them on to a cooling rack.

Sesame toast

Serves 6

6 slices of bread, brown or white, crusts cut off
75 g/3 oz butter, melted
6 tsps sesame seeds, mixed with 1 tsp salt

Brush each slice of bread both sides with melted butter. Press the salted sesame seeds into each buttered side, and toast both sides under a hot grill till the slices are golden brown. If you prefer, before toasting you can cut the bread into strips, about three per slice.

Specialist suppliers

Andy Race Fish Merchants
Mallaig
Inverness-shire
Scottish Highlands
PH41 4PX
Tel: 01687 462626
Email: sales@andyrace.co.uk
www.andyrace.co.uk

Hebridean Smokehouse
Isle of North Uist
Western Isles Clachan
Locheport
HS6 5HD
Tel: 01876 580 209
Email: sales@hebrideansmokehouse.com
www.hebrideansmokehouse.com

Isle of Skye Seafood
Isle of Skye Seafood Ltd,
Broadford
Isle of Skye
IV49 9AP
Tel: 01471 822135
Email: sales@skye-seafood.co.uk
www.skye-seafood.co.uk

Loch Bracadale Crabs
11 Eabost
Struan
Dunvegan
Isle of Skye
IV56 8FG
Tel: 01470 572264
Email: crabs@lochbracadale.co.uk

Salar Smokehouse (for hot-smoked salmon)
Lochcarban
Isle of South Uist
Outer Hebrides
HS8 5PD
Tel: 01870 610 324
Email: sales@salar.co.uk
www.salar.co.uk

Steenbergs Organic Pepper & Spice
PO Box 48
Boroughbridge
YO51 9ZW
Tel: 01765 640088
www.steenbergs.co.uk

Summer Isles Foods
Achiltibuie
Ross-shire
IV26 2YG
Tel: 01854 622353
Email: sifsalmo@globalnet.co.uk
www.summerislesfoods.com

Valvona & Crolla
Elm Row
Edinburgh
EH7 4AA
Tel: 0131 5566066
Email: sales@valvonacrolla.co.uk
www.valvonacrolla.co.uk

Index

pinhead oatmeal-coated herrings with grainy
mustard and cucumber sauce, 83–4
razor fish in oatmeal with bacon, 143
oily fish, 23
olive oil: taramasalata, 47
olives: black olive relish, 259
monkfish with tomatoes, garlic and black
olives, 202
tartare sauce, 251
omelette, smoked haddock, bacon and tomato,
92–3
onions: baked cod with onions and oranges,
105–6
mussel, onion and potato chowder, 35–6
oranges: baked cod with onions and oranges,
105–6
herring in oatmeal with orange and shallot
sauce, 131–2
orange and tomato sauce, 263
oysters stir-fried with ginger and spring onions, 64

Parmesan pastry, 95
parsley: baked fillet of cod with bacon and broad
beans in parsley sauce, 107–8
baked haddock with parsley, garlic and lemon
pesto, 117–18
butter and parsley fried trout with lemon, 159
chive, parsley and Dijon vinaigrette, 255
cod baked with parsley and lemon pesto,
186–7
horseradish and parsley sauce messine, 269
smoked haddock, lime and parsley mousse,
77–8
squid with garlic and parsley, 63
parsnip and smoked fish cakes, 171–2
pasta: pasta au gratin with smoked haddock, bacon
and leeks, 129–30
smoked fish and spinach lasagne, 169–70
spaghetti with crab, garlic, chilli, lemon and
parsley, 188–9
spaghetti with mussels, tomatoes and capers,
137–8
pastry, Parmesan, 95
pâtés: flaked smoked mackerel and apple and
chive pâté, 50
prawn, bacon and cream cheese pâté, 51–2
sardine and mushroom pâté, 48–9

smoked mackerel pâté, 46
peas: chargrilled monkfish with braised lettuce,
peas and spring onions, 205–6
roast streaky bacon-wrapped monkfish, with
peas and mint, 196–7
pecan bread roulades, smoked salmon with, 60
peppers: avocado salsa, 260
grilled plaice with red pepper, chive and parsley
dressing, 139–40
monkfish, stir-fried with red peppers, lemongrass, ginger and garlic, 198–9
roast red pepper and balsamic vinegar sauce,
258
roast red pepper, chilli and tomato fish stew,
173
steam-baked sea bass, with roast red peppers
stuffed with cannellini beans, 225–6
pesto: baked cod with spiced lentils and coriander
pesto, 111–12
baked haddock with parsley, garlic and lemon
pesto, 117–18
cod baked with parsley and lemon pesto,
186–7
pies: coulibiac of salmon, 212–13
fish pie, 176–8
salmon, tomato and basil filo parcels,
216–17
shrimp puff pie, 229
smoked haddock and spinach cheese pie,
121–2
pilchards, 23
pine nuts: baked cod with spiced lentils and
coriander pesto, 111–12
pinhead oatmeal-coated herrings with grainy
mustard and cucumber sauce, 83–4
plaice, 23
grilled plaice with red pepper, chive and parsley
dressing, 139–40
potatoes: creamy smoked haddock soup, 31–2
fish pie, 176–8
mussel, onion and potato chowder, 35–6
salmon, wild garlic and potato soup, 33
smoked haddock and spinach cheese pie,
121–2
smoked haddock fishcakes, 94
potted crab, 53
potted shrimps, 56